VIRGINIA WINERIES
YOUR COMPLETE TOUR GUIDE

Text and Photographs by Faye Weems

Foreword by Warren Winiarski

Auburn Mills • Richmond, Virginia

Virginia Wineries: Your Complete Tour Guide

Text and Graphics Copyright © 2001 by Faye Chewning Weems.
Photographs Copyright © 2001 by Faye Chewning Weems, or as otherwise credited.
Foreword Copyright © 2001 by Warren Winiarski.

All rights reserved. No part of this book may be reproduced by any means, in any format or medium, either temporarily or permanently, without the prior written permission of the publisher.

Back Cover: Grapes prefer steep slopes, rocky soils, and breathtaking views—like this one at Dye's Vineyards in far southwest Virginia.
Inside Back Cover: Wooden trellises at Wintergreen Winery.
Title Page: Dogwoods herald a new vintage cycle at Linden Vineyards.
Dedication Page: October, Horton Vineyards. These Cabernet Franc are just one of the many European varieties of wine grapes being grown successfully in Virginia today.

Library of Congress Control Number: 2001089699

ISBN 0-9710985-0-6 (Hardcover)
ISBN 0-9710985-1-4 (Paperbound)

Printed in Hong Kong

10 9 8 7 6 5 4 3 2 1

Published by   Auburn Mills Ltd.
                P.O. Box 9634
                Richmond, Virginia 23228
                www.auburnmills.com

This book is dedicated to

Thomas Jefferson,

who believed the Colonies were capable of governing themselves

—and that you could grow European grapes in Virginia.

Before embarking on your virtual tour of Virginia's wineries through the pages of this book, please take a moment to acknowledge—along with me—the many who have made the trip possible.

The following people played indispensable roles in the progress of this work by inspiring, encouraging, editing, assisting, cooperating, or indulging:

The Virginia winegrowers, winemakers, and winery staffs;
Dave Everette; Terry Simmons;
Judy Griffin; Bruce Muncy;
Shelly Adair; Thomas Weems;
Neal Hanchey; Barbara Travers;

—and above all, Patrick Duffeler. Without his guidance and support—from initial concept to the conclusion of this project—you would not be holding this book or reading these words.

Evening, springtime. A setting sun profiles the coming vintage at Breaux Vineyards.

Contents

Foreword	6	Stonewall Vineyards and Winery	52	Spotted Tavern Winery	94
Map	7			Swedenburg Estate Vineyard	96
Introduction	8	White Hall Vineyards	54	Tarara Vineyard and Winery	98
Virginia Wineries		Wintergreen Winery	58	Unicorn Winery	100

Central Region

Eastern Region

Willowcroft Farm Vineyards — 102

Afton Mountain Vineyards	14	Ingleside Plantation Vineyards	60		

Shenandoah Valley Region

Barboursville Vineyards	16				
Burnley Vineyards	20	Lake Anna Winery	64	Deer Meadow Vineyard	104
Dominion Wine Cellars	22	The Williamsburg Winery	66	Landwirt Vineyard	106
Grayhaven Winery	24	Windy River Winery	70	North Mountain Vineyard and Winery	108
Hill Top Berry Farm	26				

Northern Region

Horton Cellars Winery	28	Breaux Vineyards	72	Shenandoah Vineyards	110

Southwest Region

Jefferson Vineyards	32	Farfelu Vineyards	74		
Mountain Cove Vineyards	34	Gray Ghost Winery	76	Château Morrisette	112
Oakencroft Vineyard and Winery	36	Hartwood Winery	78	Dye's Vineyards and Winery	116
		Linden Vineyards	80	Tomahawk Mill Winery	118
Prince Michel de Virginia	38	Loudoun Valley Vineyards	82	Valhalla Vineyards	120
Rebec Vineyards	42	Naked Mountain Vineyard	84	Villa Appalaccia Winery	122
Rockbridge Vineyard	44	Oasis Winery	86	More Virginia Wineries	124
Rose River Vineyards	46	Piedmont Vineyards and Winery	90	Glossary	125
Sharp Rock Vineyards	48			Bibliography/Index	126
Stone Mountain Vineyards	50	Shadwell-Windham Winery	92	Meredyth Vineyards	128

FOREWORD

This is an illuminating and fascinating book about the wineries of Virginia—and more importantly about the people who give them life. From its stories, one is easily reminded of what Robert Louis Stevenson wrote many years ago about the Napa Valley. In his *Silverado Squatters,* Stevenson compared winegrowers to prospectors—searching in the soil for the hidden treasures to bring forth in their grapes and wines.

> Vine-planting is like the beginning of mining for the precious metals: the wine-grower also "prospects." One corner of land after another is tried with one kind of grape after another. This is a failure; that is better; a third best. So, bit by bit, they grope about for their Clos Vougeot and Lafite. Those lodes and pockets of earth, more precious than the precious ores, that yield inimitable fragrance and soft fire; those virtuous Bonanzas, where the soil has sublimated under sun and stars to something finer, and the wine is bottled poetry: these still lie undiscovered. . . . there they bide their hour, awaiting their Columbus; and nature nurses and prepares them.

Faye Weems has focused her light-beam of interest on this passionate devotion as she reveals the human, existential story of each of her pioneer Virginia winegrowers. She wants to enlighten us about that peculiar mixture of discovery, love and energy that—at best—only partially explains the quest of these winegrowers.

Most of the winegrowers she speaks about left other and earlier ways of life in order to invoke the beauty that comes from their soils and their grapes. So the book, as a whole, lets us see not only what these winegrowers do through their "products" (they are more like "offspring"), but also to see into that inward spring of energy and vision, the possession of which gives direction to everything they do in their specific location in Virginia.

These stories of vision are helpfully preceded by the author's description of the major choices available to the modern winegrowers of Virginia. Thomas Jefferson is himself enormously influential—and inspirational—in this context because of his decades-long, though unsuccessful, attempt to grow the European vinifera grape and his eventual recognition of the hybrid and American varieties as viable alternatives for these native lands.

Today, with more knowledge and in favorable places, these later Virginians are experiencing long awaited success with the fastidious vinifera species. Others have given themselves the challenge of producing American hybrid wines which vie with their European cousins for excellence and pleasure giving.

Both visions aim at achieving Jefferson's prophecy: "We could," he wrote in 1808, "in the United States, make as great a variety of wines as are made in Europe, not exactly the same kinds, but doubtless as good."

While serving as president of the International Wine & Spirits Competition in London this year, I have suggested that many of Virginia's wineries have their wines judged at an international level. I did that because it was my impression, when I was a judge at the Governor's Cup competition, that in each of the main types grown in Virginia, many wines had transcended their regional virtues and could be judged on a world stage.

I recommend this book to the general reader as a glimpse into the winegrowing lives of the people who brought about that transcendence.

Warren Winiarski
Founding Winemaker & Proprietor
Stag's Leap Wine Cellars
Napa Valley, California
May 11, 2001

Wine being among the earliest luxuries in which we indulge ourselves, it is desirable it should be made here and we have every soil, aspect & climate of the best wine countries.

— Thomas Jefferson

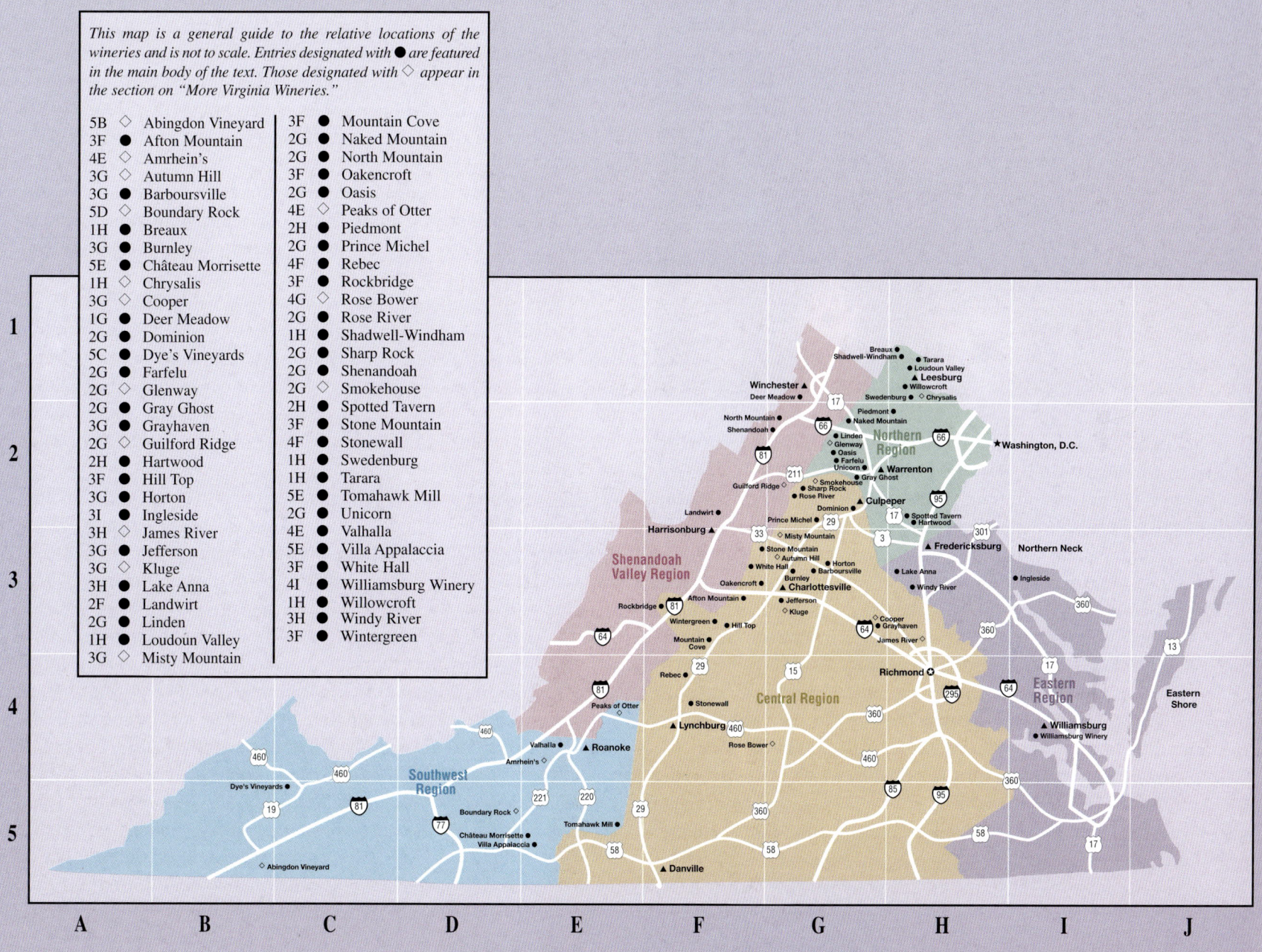

This map is a general guide to the relative locations of the wineries and is not to scale. Entries designated with ● are featured in the main body of the text. Those designated with ◇ appear in the section on "More Virginia Wineries."

5B	◇ Abingdon Vineyard		3F	● Mountain Cove
3F	● Afton Mountain		2G	● Naked Mountain
4E	◇ Amrhein's		2G	● North Mountain
3G	◇ Autumn Hill		3F	● Oakencroft
3G	● Barboursville		2G	● Oasis
5D	● Boundary Rock		4E	◇ Peaks of Otter
1H	● Breaux		2H	● Piedmont
3G	● Burnley		2G	● Prince Michel
5E	● Château Morrisette		4F	● Rebec
1H	● Chrysalis		3F	● Rockbridge
3G	◇ Cooper		4G	● Rose Bower
1G	● Deer Meadow		2G	● Rose River
2G	● Dominion		1H	● Shadwell-Windham
5C	● Dye's Vineyards		2G	● Sharp Rock
2G	● Farfelu		2G	● Shenandoah
2G	◇ Glenway		2G	● Smokehouse
2G	● Gray Ghost		2H	● Spotted Tavern
3G	● Grayhaven		3F	● Stone Mountain
2G	◇ Guilford Ridge		4F	● Stonewall
2H	● Hartwood		1H	● Swedenburg
3F	● Hill Top		1H	● Tarara
3G	● Horton		5E	● Tomahawk Mill
3I	● Ingleside		2G	● Unicorn
3H	◇ James River		4E	◇ Valhalla
3G	● Jefferson		5E	● Villa Appalaccia
3G	◇ Kluge		3F	● White Hall
3H	● Lake Anna		4I	● Williamsburg Winery
2F	● Landwirt		1H	◇ Willowcroft
2G	● Linden		3H	● Windy River
1H	● Loudoun Valley		3F	● Wintergreen
3G	◇ Misty Mountain			

Introduction

Wine is the most elegant of consumable goods. It enchants its admirers with the multiplicity of its charms, appealing to all the senses. Clad in regal hues of gold and purple, it has for centuries graced the nobleman's feast and transfigured the yeoman's supper. There is no other product about which people having nothing whatsoever to do with its manufacture are as eager to become experts. About what other commodity, liquid or otherwise, has so much been written and so much been read by so many who have never made, and will never make, a single drop themselves?

No matter how magnificent the meal it accompanies, how delicately and deliciously wrought each course in the banquet, it is the wine we hold up to the light to savor its beauty in the glass; the wine for which we seek the perfect words with which to describe and celebrate its merits; the wine with which we propose our sentiments of gratitude, remembrance, or praise. It is the *wine* that we linger over and try to understand.

The mysteries of the grape are many, of which a highly developed aptitude for flavor mimicry is one of its most fascinating, appreciated, and exploited. The thousands of different flavors that have so far been identified in the things we eat are derived from discrete chemical compounds—in the flesh of fruits, vegetables, and animals—that create specific, discernable sensations in our nose and on our palate. Closely related foods—apples and pears, for example—share closely related flavors. The kiwi fruit, on the other hand, exhibits in a single bite strong kinship with the strawberry, the lime, and the banana—three fruits with which, to look at it, it appears to have little in common. Taking together the many varieties from which wine is made, the grape exceeds all other edible substances in the number of flavors that it imitates. The question becomes then—as one Virginia winemaker posed it—whether it's the grape that is imitating all the others, or everything else that is mimicking the grape.

Either way it appears that wine, for some mysterious reason, has been uniquely fashioned to be the perfect accompaniment to just about any food we would care to eat, prepared in any pleasing way man can devise for presenting it.

Under very ordinary circumstances wine will make itself. Once the skins have been broken, wild, or native, yeasts living on the skins will start the process of fermentation in ripened grapes, or any other fruit. This spontaneous conversion of sugar to alcohol is what sends wasps and yellow jackets imbibing under the apple tree in autumn into slower but even more erratic flight patterns than when they're sober.

But wine, good wine, is much more than grape juice with alcohol. It is the culmination of a long series of processes, involving an equally long list of decisions—from selection of the varieties of grapes to grow and the soils in which to plant them to the time, if any, the wine will spend in an oak barrel and the specific forest from which the oak will have come. It relies on the use of chemical analysis in the laboratory for evaluating the levels of complex and esoteric compounds in the wine and finely calibrated tools employed right in the vineyard for measuring simpler things like sugar content in the grapes. It can all seem very calculated and very scientific, but in fact it is pure art. Just as a painter can take empty canvasses and a palette of basic colors and create pictures that are different from those that any other painter could conceive, so too can the winemaker produce an infinitely personal expression of wines. Herein lie the beauty and the mystery and the art of winemaking. An unhurried tour of Virginia wine country is a leisurely visit in a fine art gallery.

The story of grape growing in Virginia is almost 400 years old. The history of a vigorous and sustainable wine industry in Virginia, however, did not get underway until the 1970s. Before then winegrowing in this state was a mere footnote, if even that, in the memory of the majority of Virginians themselves. Perhaps the best way to undertake a necessarily brief excursion into this history is to look at the four types of grapevines that have grown here—in the order in which they first appeared on the Virginia landscape.

NATIVE AMERICAN GRAPES. When the first English settlers arrived on this continent in 1607—landing at a place they called Jamestown—they found wild grapes growing in profusion in the forests and along the banks of the rivers and the streams. More than 600 years earlier the Vikings had told an enormous fib when they advertised that chunk of ice lying just off the coast of North America as *Green*land. But they weren't lying about the stretch of shoreline they discovered—somewhere between present-day Newfoundland and Virginia—which they dubbed *Vine*land.

By the time the colonists got here, England—which produced next to none herself—had already been for quite some time a voracious, if captive, market for the wines of Europe. Within two years of disembarking, the Englishmen at Jamestown were eagerly pressing native American grapes and making their own wine. The results, however, were utterly disappointing. The wine had a flavor all its own that has come to be termed "foxy," an almost overpowering aroma component entirely unlike the more refined flavors of the familiar vintages of France, Germany, and Spain. It wasn't what they were accustomed to and the men disdained to drink it.

VITIS VINIFERA. The logical assumption on the part of the early colonists—and especially of the commercial interests who funded their expeditions to the newly discovered territories—was that if native vines, unaided by the solicitous husbandry of men, could grow as abundantly as they did in the Virginia wilds, then surely European grapes carefully planted in vineyards and diligently tended would do even better. Thus began, around 1619, the first importations of *Vitis vinifera* to America.

Vitis is the Latin word for vine. *Vini* refers, of course, to wine, and the suffix *fera* was the ancient Romans' way of saying "bearing" or "producing." Thus in *Vitis vinifera* we have the all-signifying term "vine that produces wine"—the implication for all other species of grape being obvious.

The classic wines of Europe are all made from vinifera, the ancient wine grapes that originated somewhere in Asia Minor and spread via trade, conquest, or migratory birds into Greece, Italy, Spain, Portugal, France, Germany, and beyond. They include such familiar varieties of today as Cabernet Sauvignon, Merlot, Chardonnay, Riesling, and Sangiovese. The French have been cultivating *Vitis vinifera* since the time of Christ. When it comes to yielding superb wines, this family's credentials are impeccable, and one would think that the New World, like the European lands of the Old World, would have greeted its members with arms outflung.

But in the early 1600s it was hardly a welcome wagon that came out to meet the new arrivals. What they, like early immigrants to so many places, found instead was hostility with a vengeance—a none too subtle invitation to go away and don't come back. A host of plagues—to which the native grapes had become largely immune over the ages—ganged up on the newcomers to let them know in no uncertain terms that this territory was already taken. Periodic droughts—which still harass the modern Virginia farmer—claimed the lives of young vines before their roots could grow to reach the reservoir of life-sustaining water deep within the earth. Others survived for several years only to be plucked from the vineyard of the living by the icy fingers of a bitterly cold winter. All sorts of diseases of vine and leaf and berry—many of them associated with Virginia's infamous summertime humidity—first disfigured then destroyed crop after crop, year after year.

But of all the agents sent to turn back the invasion of *Vitis vinifera* from the shores of North America, none was more relentless or efficient in its duties than phylloxera. All but invisible to the naked eye, this infinitesimally small root louse was coexisting in a state of détente with the native Virginia grapes, confining its less life-threatening damage above ground, on the leaves of the plants. The wild American grapes had long ago gotten an evolutionary jump on the louse by developing extremely hard roots as a foil against the insect's subterranean attacks.

By comparison the roots of the pampered vinifera were as soft as the hands of Europe's elite, who drank the most exquisite wines from the most elaborate goblets. In no time at all, phylloxera went underground, to drain the very life out of the hapless European vines.

The English, however, were loath to cry uncle. They tenaciously clung to the hope of not only freeing themselves from dependence on European vintners for their own wines but of becoming competitors themselves in the lucrative international wine trade. They tried everything, from importing vignerons from the winegrowing countries of Europe to plant and tend the vineyards and supervise the winemaking to "encouraging" grape growing by passing statutes mandating the cultivation of grapes by the settlers. The legislators even resorted to the unworthy tactic of rewarding those who snitched on their fellow colonists for failing to obey these laws—laws with which no less an authority than Nature herself would not permit them to comply. Everybody and everything—except the vines themselves, it would appear—were blamed for the failure. Meanwhile, tobacco grew like weeds.

More than 150 years after the settlers had crushed and pressed their first native grapes, members of the Virginia General Assembly, meeting in the colonial capital of Williamsburg, were still hopeful. They authorized money for the purchase of 100 acres in adjacent York County for establishing a vineyard and hired a professional winegrower from France to manage the project. This government-funded viticultural program was ambitious for its time, and the legislators' hopes were high, but in 1776, in the face of incontrovertible failure, the experiment was abandoned. (By contrast, today's state-supported viticultural and vinicultural programs—through Virginia Tech—are having unqualified success.)

Some dreams die hard, though, and at almost the same time that Virginia's lawmakers were giving up on viniferas, Thomas Jefferson, one of the Colonies' foremost visionaries, was planting them on land he had deeded to an Italian agronomist, Filippo Mazzei, for specifically this purpose. Mazzei—who left in 1778, with Jefferson's blessing, on a revolutionary fund-raising mission to Italy—is something of an icon in Virginia's viticultural history, even though it's fairly certain that he never produced any wine from vinifera grapes while he was in this country. In recent years modern winemakers from his native Italy have made good on Mazzei's assertions at vineyards closely associated with Thomas Jefferson. Mazzei firmly believed that Virginia had the right soils and the right climate for cultivating European grapes. At this point in the course of events of the new nation, however, there were far more pressing matters to be dealt with than establishing a winegrowing industry in Virginia.

For several decades Jefferson tried, without success, to grow palatable wine on his estate at Monticello. Why was he so absorbed with the idea of a viable wine industry in Virginia? Certainly the apparent suitability of the climate and the geography made it a challenge that had to be met, despite the altogether maddening—and in some ways inexplicable—refusal of the grapes to go along with the scheme.

Of no less importance was the fact that Jefferson himself was a great appreciator and connoisseur of fine wines. He has been quoted as saying, "Good wine is a necessity of life for me." His travels in France as ambassador to that country from 1785 to 1789 did nothing to diminish this appreciation. Jefferson, the man of ideas, was a practical thinker—an avid indulger in the pleasures to be derived from reducing the abstract to the concrete. The lofty pursuits of music and literature were ends in themselves, but time spent in thought at the drawing board manifested itself more solidly in the construction of Monticello, one of the most beautiful historic homes in America. Hours devoted to planning his farming operation were later richly rewarded at the table. Gardening yielded pleasures for the eye, the nose, and even the ear. Jefferson was without question a connoisseur of beauty. Why shouldn't the man who had penned the Declaration of Independence, one of the most beautiful and inspiring pieces of prose ever written, be inspired to grow beautiful wines on his plantation in Virginia?

THE AMERICAN HYBRIDS. An invasion, whether it is ultimately successful or not, almost always involves a certain amount of interbreeding between the would-be conquerors and the local population. While the Virginians—and later other colonists as well—were trying to establish vineyards of purebred European varieties, fraternization was occurring with natural regularity between newly planted *Vitis vinifera* and the untamed, indigenous grapes of the East Coast. The wild-growing *Vitis riparia, V. labrusca, V. aestivalis,* and *V. rotundifolia* were principle American partners in these liaisons. Of their offspring, the most likely, in fact the only, ones to survive under the stern and indiscriminate laws of natural selection were the ones that carried within them those genes of their American parent that made them resistant to disease and pests, especially phylloxera—those vines, in other words, that inherited tough roots. From among these survivors, those that ultimately flourished under the less harsh but very discriminating laws of human selection were the ones that also exhibited the more desirable traits of their European parent—more refined and complex flavors in particular.

Species enhancement through genetic manipulation became an occupation of many viticulturists in this country during the first half of the nineteenth century—but the earliest American hybrids

were discovered rather than deliberately engineered. Controlled experimentation, by the way, is fine, but unplanned incidents of cross-pollination can lead to unfortunate surprises in the vineyard. For this reason, winegrowers have long preferred to propagate cuttings taken from existing vines instead of planting seeds or seedlings.

Ultimately persuaded that vinifera could not prosper in the States, Thomas Jefferson came to hang his hopes for an American wine industry on the hybrid Alexander, a mix of a variety of vinifera and the wild *Vitis labrusca,* whose family also includes the most widely recognized American wine grape—and popular table grape as well—the deep purple Concord. But it was the Norton that was to become the most important variety for Virginia. Perfectly suited to the region's climate, this hybrid was discovered around 1835 and is a cross between *Vitis vinifera* and the native *V. aestivalis.*

In the 1850s the state's commercial wine production, based on American hybrids, was at its highest level. Within a decade the Civil War—waged in the Old Dominion like nowhere else—had resulted in the loss, through forced neglect or outright destruction, of many of Virginia's vineyards. Nevertheless, by the 1870s Virginia claret—made primarily from the Norton—had achieved considerable renown in both Europe and America. Unfortunately, prohibition sentiments were on a steadily upward curve, and in 1914, five years before Congress made it nationwide, Virginia's legislature voted the entire state dry—bringing a 300-year-old aspiration to an abrupt end. Over the next half century, despite the repeal of Prohibition, the notion of Virginia as a significant wine producing region all but vanished from the state's collective consciousness.

FRENCH HYBRIDS AND THE RETURN OF VITIS VINIFERA. Towards the end of the nineteenth century, phylloxera—the deadly root louse that had made it virtually impossible for vinifera vines to survive for any length of time on the East Coast—came within a hairs-breadth of completely wiping France off the grape growing map. Hybrids were developed by French viticulturists as a less expensive alternative to the grafting of vinifera vines onto American rootstock as a means of combating the decimating plague—which had been accidentally imported from America. French hybrids were crosses between vinifera and the less "foxy" American species *Vitis riparia* (as opposed to the much foxier *V. labrusca*) and actually became quite popular in France. They didn't show up in America until the late 1940s, and it wasn't until the 1960s that Virginia began to take notice.

Successes in other mid-Atlantic states finally ignited the lamp of viticultural memory in the Old Dominion, and in the late sixties and the seventies farmers began planting American and French hybrids, of which the French varieties soon claimed most of the Virginia acreage devoted to winegrowing. Among the most popular were the Seyval Blanc, the Vidal Blanc, and the Chambourcin.

In the 1980s Virginians once again dared to plant vinifera grapes. Some brave souls—pioneers at vineyards like Barboursville in central Virginia and Piedmont, Oasis, and Meredyth in northern Virginia—had actually set out a few vinifera varieties in the seventies.

Today vinifera vines—European cuttings, that is, grafted onto American rootstock—account for the overwhelming majority of wine grape production in Virginia. In almost parable-like fashion, the wild American grape—the long-despised native vine—eventually became the only means by which Eastern grape growers, including Virginians, were able to create the European-style wines they and their vinicultural forebears had, for nearly four centuries, yearned to produce.

New plantings of vinifera in Virginia continue to outstrip new acreage in hybrids by an ever-widening margin. Some growers are puzzled by the rush on the part of others to totally exclude the French hybrids in favor of the vinifera. After all, the hybrid vines were, by and large, the bootstraps by which Virginia's wine industry pulled itself up again after being flat on its back for nearly sixty years. Some very estimable wines are being made here from the likes of the

Chambourcin and the Seyval Blanc. And in my travels across this entire state—talking with winemakers and tasting their wines—I can honestly say I never met a late harvest Vidal I didn't like. Nevertheless, one cannot deny the Virginia winegrowers their due or their destiny, and that seems to be to become world-class producers of classic European-style wines from *Vitis vinifera.*

While his early efforts were devoted to vinifera, eventually Thomas Jefferson came to conclude that successful winegrowing in Virginia, and the nation, would rely upon the cultivation of American hybrids. The number of European varietals that now top the lists of wineries across the state and the flood of national and international awards being bestowed upon vinifera wines from Virginia prove that the initial instincts of Jefferson—and the early colonists as well— were indeed correct.

Winegrowing here still is not easy. Modern cures for ancient ills keep mildew, fungus, and other scourges in check, but it's a constant battle between the dogged determination of the farmer and the unrelenting challenges of nature. Virginia—while her climate is conducive—is not like California, which has the most cooperative grape growing climate in the country. Viticulturally speaking, Virginia is a region of microclimates, and extreme care has to be taken to choose precisely the right site to match the specific variety of grape to be planted. There are far more vineyards in the state than there are wineries. Most winery owners simply do not have enough contiguous acres suitable for grape growing to meet their production needs. A 600-acre property may have only 100 acres that meet the strict requirements of the fastidious wine grape.

A journey into Virginia wine country will take you deep into the cultural and political history of the Old Dominion, the most historical state in the Union. The winegrowers make the most of their local cultural connections, weaving them into the names of their wines and of the wineries themselves. Civil War buffs will be richly rewarded on their trips to the grape growing regions of northern Virginia and the Shenandoah Valley. Fans of the third president will enjoy visiting the wineries of central Virginia, whose nexus is Thomas Jefferson's own Charlottesville. Williamsburg, with nearby Jamestown, offers the chance to immerse yourself in not only America's colonial past but her earliest viticultural history as well.

The more than sixty wineries that currently operate in Virginia are spread across the entire state. There are pockets of activity, however, and for your excursion-planning convenience the wineries in this book have been organized into five regions—the same as those in the annual *Virginia Wineries Festival and Tour Guide* published by the Virginia Wine Marketing Program and available for free at the wineries or by contacting the Marketing Office at the address and phone number referenced in the bibliography.

The map provided with this text can best be described as stylized and is meant to give only a general idea of the relative locations of the wineries. If you're planning to take in several wineries in a day, allow yourself plenty of time to get from one to the other. Always bear in mind that a Virginia country mile is longer than an interstate mile—and a mountain mile is considerably longer than a country mile. Keep a navigational eye out for the red and green winery tour (grape cluster) signs as you near your destination, and drive at a pace that will allow you to fully enjoy the stretches of scenic beauty you'll encounter along the way.

It's been proven, at least empirically, that only change is constant, and so it is with something as young and dynamic as Virginia's modern winemaking industry. This book is, therefore, what its name implies—a guide. While the information presented is as accurate as could be ascertained at the time of publication, the hours of operation and other aspects related to your visit to the winery are, as is the case with any place of business, subject to change.

At the wineries you will sample Virginia wines in surroundings that run the gamut from the simplest ad hoc arrangements amid the sometimes leisurely, sometimes intense activity of actual wine production to some of the most elegantly appointed tasting rooms to be entered on either the East Coast or the West. While many of the physical winemaking plants are extremely interesting from an architectural and historical point of view, a book about Virginia wineries is less about stunning architecture and more about exceptional wines and pioneering winegrowers. The people who actually make the wine range from the self-taught sole proprietor of the business to professionally trained winemakers with no stake in the winery other than their own reputations.

The styles of winemaking you'll encounter in Virginia are as diverse as the individual winemakers themselves. There's more than one philosophy about tannins, for instance, with some giving freer rein to the mouth-puckering quality of a varietal like Cabernet

Sauvignon, while others want to soften the astringent nature of red wines as much as possible. Even when they agree on what the end results should be, winemakers often employ completely different—sometimes seemingly contradictory—methods for achieving them. Often individual style is not so much a matter of arriving at a different place with the wine as it is of getting to the same place from entirely different directions.

Whether to whole-cluster press the grapes; whether to fine and filter the wine; what degree of malolactic conversion is just right for the Chardonnay; whether to oak or not to oak and if so, whether to do it in French, American, or Hungarian barrels—these methods and these decisions are dependent on a number of things: the preferences of the winemaker, the size of the operation, the makeup of the vintage, the vicissitudes of nature. Ultimately the decision as to which styles are the most pleasing is entirely up to you.

There are many places to buy Virginia wines: Major festivals bring virtually the entire industry together at one time in one place several times a year, and numerous regional and local events offer the opportunity to simultaneously compare the wines of more than one winery. The *Festival and Tour Guide* mentioned earlier includes a full calendar of events from January through December. Local wines can be enjoyed with a meal at Virginia's finer restaurants, many of which are continually expanding an already considerably long Virginia wine list. You will find Virginia wines at retail outlets like grocery stores, wine shops, major discount marts, and the state-operated ABC stores, which carry Virginia wines exclusively.

But the best place to purchase Virginia wine is at the winery itself. Here you not only get to taste the wine before you buy, you will also learn something about wine and winemaking (and no matter how much you already know, there's always something new to learn), and at the smaller wineries especially, you will often have a chance to meet and talk directly with the owner or the winemaker or both.

If Thomas Jefferson, a man of incalculable intellect, had been able to divine all its causes and devise all the remedies to treat the failure of *Vitis vinifera* to thrive in the eastern United States, agricultural Virginia today would—in the opinion of one winemaker I talked with—look like France. While the notion may stretch the imagination, it is certainly true that winegrowing as a force for economic good in this state would be at least two hundred years ahead of where it is now.

But never mind, everything in its time, and no one, not even Thomas Jefferson, could expect all his dreams to be realized in his own lifetime. Virginia's modern winegrowers are fulfilling his dream, and it should come as no surprise to anyone that these Virginians—whether they were born and raised here or came here from somewhere else—take this legacy and this vision of Mr. Jefferson's very much to heart.

You are cordially welcome in Virginia wine country. Please visit with us often. May the enjoyment of our fine wines be something you look forward to with growing anticipation—and may you partake of their pleasures with increasing regularity. Thomas Jefferson would consider it a personal favor if you did.

Faye Weems

Afton Mountain Vineyards

Afton Mountain Vineyards
234 Vineyard Lane
Afton, VA 22920

Hours: 10 a.m. to 6 p.m. every day except Tuesday from March through October; 10 a.m. to 5 p.m. November and December. Open from 10 a.m. to 5 p.m. Friday through Monday in January and February. Closed New Year's Day, Easter, Thanksgiving, and Christmas.

Directions: From **Staunton** take I-64 east to exit 99. Go east on Rte. 250 for 1.3 miles, east on Rte. 6 for 1.7 miles, south on Rte. 631 for 1.2 miles. From **Charlottesville** take I-64 west to exit 107. Go west on Rte. 250 for 6 miles, south on Rte. 151 for 3 miles, west on Rte. 6 for 1.8 miles, south on Rte. 631 for 1.2 miles.

Phone: 540-456-8667
Fax: 540-456-8002

Tasting fee: None, except $3 per person for groups over 20 (Includes souvenir glass.)

Wines: Chardonnay, Gewürztraminer, Pinot Noir, Riesling, Cabernet Sauvignon, *Sweet Afton*

Wine related items for sale? Yes
Picnic area? Yes
Food available? Light snacks
Special Programs? Afton Mountain Wine Alliance

Owners: Tom and Shinko Corpora
Winemaker: Shinko Corpora
Viticulturist: Tom Corpora

This winery is named after the most notorious mountain in Virginia. As winemaker Shinko Corpora points out, Afton Mountain as a discrete entity on any official map does not actually exist. A sense of the unreal can indeed envelop travelers on Interstate 64 as they feel their way through the legendary fog that often settles on its summit.

The tiny town of Afton is certainly on your map, though, just a few miles after you leave its unofficial namesake mountain at Exit 99 near Waynesboro. It's in the picturesque Rockfish Valley, as is the fifty-two-acre farm that Shinko and husband Tom Corpora purchased in 1988. This was shortly after he left a distinguished career in journalism, first with UPI and then NBC News. Tom grew up on the other side of the country, in Los Angeles, and Shinko—a former language instructor with the Berlitz Schools—on the other side of the world, in Japan.

When the Corporas bought the property, it already had six acres of vineyards and a winery, but both the vines and the winemaking had been neglected for several years. The couple spent the next two seasons rehabilitating the grapevines and the next seven refurbishing and upgrading the winery.

One of the first things they did was to enlarge the retail area. The stone facade that was once part of an outside wall is now on the inside, behind the bar in the new tasting room. The all-vinifera wines to be sampled here appeal to both the oak enthusiast and those who, like Afton Mountain's winemaker, prefer the distinctive endowments of the individual grape varieties over the more general contributions of the barrel. Most of Shinko's wines are fermented to dryness, but *Sweet Afton*—a dessert wine blend of Riesling, Muscat, and Gewürztraminer—flows as gently on the taster's palate as the Scottish poet's river among its green braes.

Small tables set against picture windows in the tasting room offer an unobstructed view of neatly laid out, fully recuperated vines in the foreground and nicely arranged, densely forested mountains in the background. If you come in on a chilly day, stop and warm yourself by the stove on the raised hearth in the corner. If the fire gets low, there are plenty of logs in the wood pile outside on the crush pad.

Either before or after you sample their wines—they're somewhat informal up here in the mountains—take a tour of the production area. Afton Mountain is one of a number of wineries in Virginia that employ a gravity-flow system in their winemaking process. The first tier is on the ground level and can be entered from the tasting room or the crush pad. It is basically a catwalk that overlooks stainless steel fermentation and storage tanks one level below. Trap doors in the metal bridge are positioned directly over the tanks. When Shinko is making red wines, the crusher/destemmer is placed over a manhole and the must (the grape juice and skins), rather than being pumped, is funneled into a stainless steel tank. After complete or partial fermentation has taken place, the juice is pressed off the skins and allowed to flow into oak barrels on the lowest level.

A ninety-six-foot-long man-made cave provides a dark, cool environment for Shinko's oaked wines while they get better with age in a mix of French and American barrels—French for the white wines and American for the reds. The far end opens onto the picnic area and an impressive view of mountains and vineyards.

The Corporas produce about 3,000 cases of wine a year. All of their grapes are grown on their own farm or at nearby Cardinal Point Vineyards. The vines on the winery property are planted on a southeast-facing slope, which gives them maximum exposure to the sun. According to Tom, who has primary responsibility for the vineyards, they suffer very little spring frost damage because of an accommodating device of nature called thermal inversion. Cold air flows down the mountainside to settle below the vineyards at the same time that warmer air is pushing its way up. At an elevation of 960 feet, Tom's vines are at one of Rockfish Valley's warmest spots.

Deeply rooted in a mixture of rocky clay and loam, the vines at Afton Mountain produce approximately 2½ tons of fruit per acre. If you ask Tom how many cases of wine can be squeezed out of that, he'll tell you that, on average, a ton of grapes will produce 160 gallons—but the former wordsmith leaves the arithmetic up to you. At 3.785 liters per gallon, 750 milliliters per bottle, and twelve bottles per case, the math comes out very close to 67 cases per ton, or 168 per acre.

In the winery, where cellar masters are given to talking in terms of gallon capacity, it's useful to know that a gallon is roughly four-tenths of a case, so a 1,500-gallon tank will hold about 600 cases; a standard 55-gallon barrel, 22 cases.

At the bottom of the mountain it's useful to know that once you've negotiated the long and winding road to the top, you can, if you're so inclined, coast down the paved drive past the vineyards to Tom and Shinko's winery. Here you'll find outstanding varietals and blends—dry wines and sweet wines from at least eight varieties of *Vitis vinifera,* the original European wine grape.

Barboursville Vineyards

Barboursville Vineyards
and Historic Ruins
17655 Winery Road
Barboursville, VA 22923

Hours: 10 a.m. to 5 p.m. Monday through Saturday; 11 a.m. to 5 p.m. on Sunday. Free tours are offered on Saturdays and Sundays.

Directions: From the **intersection of Rtes. 20 and 33,** take Rte. 20 south for 200 yards. Turn left onto Rte. 678 and go 1/2 mile. Turn right onto Rte. 777, then right at the first driveway and follow the signs to winery.

Phone: 540-832-3824
Fax: 540-832-7572
E-mail: bvvy@barboursvillewine.com
Website: www.barboursvillewine.com

Tasting fee: $3 per person (Includes souvenir glass.)

Wines: Cabernet Sauvignon, Cabernet Franc, Chardonnay, Merlot, Pinot Grigio, *Octagon, Phileo, Malvaxia*

Wine related items for sale? Yes
Picnic area? Yes
Food available? Full service restaurant
Facilities for private functions? Yes

Owner: Giovanni Zonin
Winemaker: Luca Paschina
Viticulturist: Fernando Franco

History is a passion with Giovanni Zonin, and if it can be linked to winemaking, so much the better. The Zonin family has been growing grapes and making wine for nearly two centuries. In 1976 the owner of the largest privately held wine company in Old World Italy was exploring Virginia, looking for possible New World sites for a vineyard. The topography and soil of the sheep farm for sale near Barboursville made it a strong candidate from a purely viticultural standpoint. What tipped the balance in its favor was its history.

In 1814 the governor of Virginia, James Barbour, began construction of a house on his plantation in Orange County near Charlottesville. His close friend Thomas Jefferson, whose second term as the nation's president had ended in 1809, was the architect. The Barboursville mansion took eight years to complete and when it was finished was, from the tax assessor's point of view, the grandest residence in the county. On the main floor there was a large octagonal room, a signature element in Jefferson's architectural style. Here the former governor and the former president—and their mutual friend former president Madison—got together on a number of occasions. As members of Virginia's aristocracy they were among the few of their era who could afford to import wines from Europe. It's easy to imagine the conversation turning at times to Jefferson's attempts—all unsuccessful—to cultivate vinifera grapes in Virginia. It was no doubt in this room that the author of the Declaration of Independence sometimes exceeded his doctor's recommendation of a glass and a half of wine a day and did, in his own words, "even treble it with a friend."

The mansion was destroyed by fire in 1884, but its ruins have been carefully preserved. Today Luca Paschina is growing vinifera grapes and making fine European-style wines in plain view of the octagonal room where Thomas Jefferson and James Barbour once talked of wine and made their toasts.

Luca received his training in Alba, the center of winemaking in the northwest region of Italy known as Piemonte—the Piedmont. After earning his degree in enology, he worked there several years, first as winemaker, then in the vineyards as viticulturist, and finally in sales and marketing. In 1990 he became a consultant to the Italian wine industry and in the same year was retained by Giovanni Zonin on a consulting basis at Barboursville. In August of 1990 he accepted a permanent position as general manager of this Italian-owned winery in the Piedmont region of Virginia.

There are currently 135 acres of vines under Luca's care on 870 acres of the former Barbour plantation. The primary varieties are Chardonnay, Pinot Grigio (Pinot Gris), Cabernet Sauvignon, and its cousin, Cabernet Franc. For years Luca has been preaching that the Franc, a relative newcomer to vineyards in this state, is the best red grape for Virginia. From his experience it's the easiest to grow, and it performs consistently well, even in seasons that are less than perfect, such as those with cool or overly wet summers. In years when the weather is cooperative, it produces a great wine. Nineteen ninety-seven was such a season, and Luca's Cabernet Franc from that vintage was proclaimed the best wine made in Virginia at the 1999 Governor's Cup competition. These days Luca is preaching to the choir. As you visit other wineries throughout the state, you'll find that enrollment is increasing in the Cabernet Franc school of thought. The softly tannic red that used to be grown primarily to blend, now shows up on more and more lists as a full-fledged varietal.

Luca, who always worked for very large companies in Italy, has adjusted well to the more relaxed manner of winemaking in Virginia. He acknowledges that regardless of size wineries share many of the same problems, but at Barboursville, he says, "we are not in a rush at least. We grow step by step, and we try not to make the step longer than our legs."

So far all of Barboursville's steps seem to have been in the right direction. This includes their strategic adaptation to the French government's limits on the export of barrel-grade oak at the annual forest auctions. Through Italian connections unique to Barboursville, Luca has cultivated a private source of premium French oak barrels from a master cooper in Piemonte. He has also identified sources of American oak barrels of dramatically improved quality. Several domestic cooperage firms that once sold mainly to the bourbon and whiskey trade—where extremely potent oak from greener wood is desirable—have completely changed their barrel-making techniques to meet the requirements of the growing number of American wine producers. Some companies hired French coopers, and others, particularly in California, joined forces with French firms and are now supplying American winemakers with excellent barrels.

The original winery here was in a brick building where the former owner's sheep were sent each spring to be divested of their winter woolens. When Barboursville's new winery and tasting room were built in 1996, the erstwhile shearing parlor became an office. Since 1999 the space has been occupied by the intimate and elegant Palladio Restaurant, named in honor of the sixteenth-century architect Andrea Palladio, whose style is often reflected in Jefferson's work.

A broad arcade runs the length of the new Tuscan-style winery. Several of its arches frame vignettes of farm buildings close by, while in others braided hills stretch their vineyard symmetry toward a ridge of mountains in the distance. Inside the tasting room, terra-cotta floor tiles and whitewashed plaster create a cool, Mediterranean-like retreat from Virginia's aggressive summer sun. A wall with wide arches and double-sided fireplace separates the gift shop area from the bar. Wine-related antiques from Italy and artifacts from the Barboursville ruins are on display around the room.

Barboursville Vineyards

The bar at this winery is very long and very straight and, except for the two extremely large Italian barrel heads on the pouring side, reminds you a little of something out of the old West. On the tasting side, besides the more traditional varieties, you can sample wines like *Malvaxia*. Made from the ancient Malvasia grape—which originated in Asia Minor—this wine found its way from France to Elizabethan England, where it was known as malmsey. The red Barbera varietal is another Barboursville specialty. They were the first Virginia winery to grow and bottle this northern Italian wine with the prominent raspberry nose. Luca's *Octagon* pays homage to Jefferson, the architect-president, in a premium blend of Merlot, Cabernet Sauvignon, and Cabernet Franc.

The tour of the ruins at Barboursville Vineyards is self-guided. It leads through a maze of slow-growing boxwood that for height vie with the columns of the three-story mansion, attesting to the age of both house and gardens. A winery docent will conduct you on your tour of Barboursville's very modern production facilities, where at harvest Luca Paschina has as many as thirty different batches of wine fermenting at once—"and every one of them needing," as he puts it, "some different treatment at just the right time. It's like having a big kitchen with thirty pots boiling and trying to make sure you don't burn any one of them."

He must not have burned too many or his name surely would not appear as viticulturist—along with those of the architect and Barboursville's owner—carved in stone over the winery's new entrance.

BURNLEY VINEYARDS

Burnley Vineyards
and Daniel Cellars
4500 Winery Lane
Barboursville, VA 22923

Hours: 11 a.m. to 5 p.m. Friday through Monday from January through March. 11 a.m. to 5 p.m. daily from April through December. Closed New Year's Day, Thanksgiving, and Christmas Day.

Directions: From the **intersection of Rtes. 20 and 33,** go south on Rte. 20 for 2 miles, turn right onto Rte. 641 and go 1/3 mile to the winery. From **Charlottesville,** go north for 15 miles on Rte. 20, turn left onto Rte 641 and go 1/3 mile to the winery.

Phone: 540-832-2828
Fax: 540-832-2280
E-mail: burnleywines@rlc.net
Website:
www.burnleywines.com

Tasting fee: $2 per person (applied to purchases during visit); $2 per person for tour (by appointment only)

Wines: Chardonnay, Riesling, Cabernet Sauvignon, Zinfandel, *Rivanna Red, Peach Fuzz, Spicy Rivanna*

Wine related items for sale? Yes
Picnic area? Yes
Facilities for private functions? Yes

Owners: C. J., Patt, Dawn, and Lee Reeder
Winemaker: Lee Reeder
Viticulturist: C. J. Reeder

Imagine that it's the middle of the night sometime in April. You have thirty acres of grapevines that have just budded out. The single leaves that have uncurled along the otherwise bare, stick-like canes are the tender beginnings of this year's crop. As the season progresses, some leaves will give rise to fruit-bearing shoots—unless a hard spring freeze descends on your vineyard, wrapping each and every leaf in a shroud of lethal cold. The forecast is for a killing frost, and in the predawn hours the alarms go off, warning you that the temperature in the vineyards has reached a critical low.

If you are Lee Reeder, you know what has to be done: get up and go start the wind machines. At an elevation of 650 feet, his vineyards are not high enough to benefit from the natural phenomenon of thermal inversion. The two powerful, twin-bladed fans are designed to simulate the effect by pulling the warmer air hovering above the vineyards down to vine level. To work, the fans have to be up where the warm air is circulating. The engine on the newer machine is at ground level, but to start the older equipment, Lee has to climb—rung by rung—thirty-five feet up the tower to reach its engine. Then, with the propeller stirring up a terrific draft, he has to climb back down. This in the dark, in the cold, in the middle of the night. Being a grape grower in Virginia is positively not for the faint of heart.

Lee and his parents, C.J. and Patt, are originally from California, where wind machines are fairly common in some winegrowing areas. Burnley Vineyards was the first in Virginia to install the equipment, which can also help prevent midwinter deep-freeze damage to the vines themselves. Barboursville Vineyards and Prince Michel, whose elevations are similar to Burnley's, soon followed suit.

The winery is located on Route 641, where there was once a bustling community called Burnley Station. The Burnleys owned a lot of land in the area during Thomas Jefferson's time, including the acreage now belonging to the Reeders, and they are still well represented in adjacent Orange County. "We're always getting customers in here," says Lee, "whose first name, last name, or middle name is Burnley."

While it probably doesn't hurt, business at the winery is not dependent upon name association but upon the quality of the wines the Reeders have been producing since 1984. Their list is diverse, with at least one varietal that is being made at only a handful of Virginia wineries. Aficionados of the pale pink wine known as white Zinfandel may be surprised to learn that this grape is actually dark purple, almost black in color. Lee's dry, full-bodied, unblended and unfiltered red Zinfandel, rich in spice and fruit, is very different from the blush wine that results when the grape is processed as a white wine, with little or no time spent on the skins to extract their intensely ruby color. In an interesting twist, Burnley is making their *Rivanna Sunset* blush from the Chambourcin, a French hybrid which enjoys popularity as a varietal with many Virginia winemakers or which they use to blend with other reds. Burnley's *Somerset* is a sweet mix of red and white wines, and here the Chambourcin shows up again, this time as the red component that gives this pink wine its rosy complexion.

Lee currently uses both French and American barrels, but like some other Virginia winemakers is shifting towards more American oak. Each barrel sees a four-year tour of duty at Burnley—two years aging white wines, then two for reds. After that, according to Lee, they make excellent planters.

Burnley produces 5,000 cases a year, varietals and blends from vinifera and French hybrid grapes. They're even growing a little of the Norton, an American hybrid that was first introduced in 1835. The Reeders have recently stepped up their plantings, and Lee expects their output to double in the next few years when all the new vines start maturing.

As is the case at most Virginia vineyards, Burnley's grapes are all harvested by hand. As the workers pick, they place the grapes in yellow boxes called lugs. When the picking is done, a gondola fitted with an auger is hooked to a tractor and driven between the rows, where workers empty the plastic containers into the moving wagon. At the winery, the auger is turned on, and the berry clusters are gently corkscrewed into the crusher/destemmer.

The property that the Reeders bought in 1976 was previously owned by a relative of Lee's wife, Dawn, whom he met while studying enology at Virginia Tech. It was all "unimproved" land, meaning that, unlike for many new winery owners in the state, there were no existing buildings—no barn, stable, or dairy—that the family could easily convert to wine production. The chalet-style facility at Burnley was constructed in stages as revenues from their expanding business allowed.

Throughout history wine has been a beverage routinely enjoyed by people at all levels of society—except in this country, where the difficulty of growing grapes early on made good wine unavailable to all but those who could afford the considerable expense of importing it. Today it's still a new experience for many people, and Lee believes it's important to create an atmosphere in which the wine neophyte can feel comfortable. You'll find no frost settling on his tasting room, where on chilly days a pot of hot, mulled *Spicy Rivanna Red* on the wood stove sends cozy aromas of cinnamon, clove, and nutmeg throughout the room. Here you'll feel right at home with the wines and the winemaker. And your name doesn't even have to be Burnley.

Dominion Wine Cellars

Dominion Wine Cellars
Number One Winery Avenue
Culpeper, VA 22701

Hours: 10 a.m. to 4:30 p.m. Monday through Saturday and 12 noon to 4:30 p.m. on Sunday. Closed Thanksgiving, Christmas, and New Year's Day.

Directions: From **Rte. 29 Bypass,** take the Culpeper exit at Rte. 3 and go west towards Culpeper. Turn right onto McDevitt Drive, then right onto Winery Avenue. From the **D.C.** area, take I-66 west to Rte. 29 south towards Culpeper and follow directions above. From **Charlottesville,** take Rte. 29 north towards Culpeper and follow directions above. From **Richmond,** take I-95 north to **Fredericksburg,** then Rte. 3 west to Culpeper. Turn right on McDevitt Drive, then right onto Winery Avenue.

Phone: 540-825-8772
Fax: 540-829-0377

Tasting fee: $1 per person

Wines: *Late Harvest Vidal, Blackberry Merlot, Raspberry Merlot, Lord Culpeper Seyval, Filippo Mazzei Reserve, East Davis Street White,* as well as varietals (Chardonnay, Cabernet) and blends from the Williamsburg Winery

Wine related items for sale? Yes
Picnic area? Yes
Food available? Light snacks
Facilities for private functions? Yes

Owner: The Williamsburg Winery Ltd.
Winemaker: Steve Warner
Viticulturist: Kevin Jones

Started by a cooperative of seventeen Virginia vineyard owners who pooled their resources to build a facility where they could bring their grapes to be crushed, pressed, and vinified, Dominion Wine Cellars is now owned by the state's largest wine producer, the Williamsburg Winery.

The group of independent growers at Dominion was extremely successful at producing quality wine grapes, but several years after opening they recognized the need for professional management expertise and turned to Williamsburg's owner, with the idea of having the eastern Virginia winery oversee operations at the cooperative.

Patrick Duffeler understood well how to organize and run a business and market its products. In 1987 his brand new winery near Colonial Williamsburg had produced 2,500 cases of wine. The next year the output jumped to 8,000 cases. By 1989 the winery was running out of inventory and the availability of fruit was lagging far behind the demand for its wines. Taking over the management of Dominion meant wine to sell now and grapes for making more in the fall. An agreement was signed between the cooperative and Williamsburg in 1990. In November of 1993 Patrick's company bought the Culpeper County winemaking enterprise outright.

There were only 2½ acres of vines at the Dominion site when Williamsburg acquired it, and the more or less experimental vineyard showed signs of having become the neglected stepchild of seventeen growers, each with his own grapes to tend. Patrick had the existing vines torn out and replaced with Vidal Blanc, this time ten acres' worth. Grapes from this vineyard now find their way into the *Governor's White* blend of Vidal and Muscat, the most popular Virginia wine on the market.

Dominion makes about 5,000 cases of wine a year, and its production capabilities are similar to those found at other midsized Virginia wineries. In the winery proper, tall, German-made stainless steel fermentation and storage tanks aspire towards a beautifully crafted cathedral ceiling. The new roof over the winery replaces the one removed suddenly by Hurricane Fran as she spiraled across the state in September 1997, raining memorable mischief on the vineyards of central and western Virginia.

Barrel aging takes place here, but there is no bottling line at Dominion. Instead the winery sends its wine to the Williamsburg facility in refrigerated tank trucks. In a similar manner, a flatbed truck is used to transport the mechanical harvester from Williamsburg to the Culpeper vineyard. To understand how this equipment works, think about what happens when you buy table grapes at the supermarket. No matter how gently you lift your carefully selected cluster from the bin, invariably a half dozen or more grapes drop right off their stems. In the vineyard the mechanical harvester moves down the rows, gently shaking the vines. The ripe grapes, riper than those in the store, fall effortlessly off the cluster into the harvester.

While Dominion shares many things with its parent company, it has always been Patrick's intention for the winery in Culpeper to retain its own identity, and a list of mainly specialty wines has evolved under the Dominion label. *Lord Culpeper* is a barrel-aged, 100 percent varietal made from the French hybrid Seyval Blanc. *Filippo Mazzei Reserve,*

named for the Italian agronomist who attempted to grow vinifera grapes for Thomas Jefferson, is a mix of Nebbiolo and Cabernet Sauvignon. Dominion was the first Virginia winery, and possibly the first in the country, to ferment grape juice and fruit juice together. Their extravagantly delicious raspberry and blackberry Merlots, both fortified dessert wines, are two of Dominion's most successful creations.

You can sample wines made in Culpeper at the Williamsburg Winery and those made in Williamsburg here at Dominion. *Plantation Blush* is a strawberry-evoking sipping wine that tasting room manager Ursula Harris calls gossiping wine—a blend of Seyval, Chambourcin, and Muscat that would pair nicely with a wide veranda and close friends on a summer afternoon.

Gossiping is permitted on the deck at Dominion, as long as it's amiable. Picnicking is permitted under the trees alongside the vineyard as long as you're content with the view. The château-style winery, with its arches and gables and enclosed courtyard, is easy on the eyes, and the soft outlines of the foothills in the distance are gentle on the nerves.

Dominion and Williamsburg still work with a number of the original co-op growers, and Patrick Duffeler is delighted with the quality of fruit coming out of their vineyards. Being able to get grapes from many different microclimates throughout Virginia is viewed as a distinct advantage at Williamsburg, whose owner believes strongly in experimenting with blends—including mixing the same variety from different vineyards—the way they do in Bordeaux. Winemaker Steve Warner gets flavors from Chardonnays grown on the state's Eastern Shore, for example, that are distinctly different from those harvested here in the Piedmont. "It's amazing," says Patrick, "what 1 or 2 percent of a wine with different aroma compounds added to the blend will do—how it will beautify the wine. That's really the extraordinary thing in winemaking." Virginia, he concludes, "will benefit from searching in the blend." To this end he has recently added a micro-winery to Steve's new office/laboratory complex in Williamsburg, where the winemaker who is making the most Virginia wine can do precisely that.

Grayhaven Winery

Grayhaven Winery
4675 E. Grey Fox Circle
Gum Spring, VA 23065

Hours: 9 a.m. to 5 p.m. Saturday and Sunday. Weekdays please call ahead. "If we're home, we're open."

Directions: From **Richmond** via I-64, take the Gum Spring exit to Rte. 250 west. Turn right onto Rte. 700, then onto Rte. 619, then Shepherd Spring Road, then Fox Chase Run, and then E. Grey Fox Circle. From **Charlottesville** via I-64, take the Hadensville exit to Rte. 250 east. Turn onto Rte. 700, then Rte. 619, then Shepherd Spring Road, Fox Chase Run, and E. Grey Fox Circle. From **points north**, take Rte. 522 south, then Rte. 619, then Shepherd Spring Road, Fox Chase Run, and E. Grey Fox Circle.

Phone: 804-556-3917
Website: www.grayhavenwinery.com

Tasting fee: None

Wines: Seyval, Vidal Blanc, Maréchal Foch, Riesling, *Eventide* (blush), *Voyager* (blended white)

Facilities for private functions: Yes

Owners: Charles and Lyn Peple
Winemakers/Viticulturists: the Peple family

To understand just how hands on the business of owning a winery can be, you need only pay a visit to this small winemaking operation in Goochland County. Charles and Lyn Peple were thinking far ahead to retirement when they purchased fifty acres in Gum Spring in 1978 with the idea of supplementing their income by propagating grapevines. While they have given a few away, "To this day," says Lyn, "we have not sold any vines." Instead they went immediately into grape production.

They have seventeen varieties altogether at Grayhaven, but the main crops are the French hybrids Seyval and Vidal and the American hybrid Cayuga. There are currently about four acres in production at the winery, with another four still maturing. The Peples are in the process of clearing an additional five acres, which they have designated for red grapes—Maréchal Foch (another French hybrid) and Cabernet Franc.

In the mid-nineties Lyn and Charles decided to stop selling their grapes to other wine producers and to start their own winery. Their first crush was in 1995. Because of bad winters the following two years, they had virtually no grapes to pick in 1996 or 1997. Almost as soon as the berries are harvested, Lyn explains, bud tissue begins to form on the vines. If temperatures shoot up unseasonably in January or February, bud formation gets ahead of itself. A sudden and severe drop in temperature can do irreparable damage to the season's vintage. In 1998, a much better year, the winery produced 400 cases, and 1999 recorded a slight increase. The plan is to remain small, as befits a retirement enterprise, and 2,000 cases a year is the current goal.

The winery, which is a work in progress near to completion, was built by the Peples themselves, with the help of their two daughters and their husbands. The windows in the tasting room came, in a roundabout way, from Lyn and Charles's previous house. When they renovated it, they installed windows that had once been in a Holiday Inn. They paid fifty dollars apiece for the windows and trimmed them out in wood. When they started construction on the winery, they heard that the new owners of their former house were doing their own remodeling and taking out the motel windows. The Peples bought the windows back. This time they paid—fifty dollars apiece. The twelve-foot window next to the spiral staircase is from a friend's art studio, and the staircase itself is out of an old ship. Stained glass windows, being designed by Charles, are planned for the tasting room and other parts of the winery.

The heart pine ceiling in the tasting room is made of siding the Peples salvaged from their own house, which is being modernized, and the pine beams came out of an abandoned warehouse in Richmond. Something that looks old while being new is the massive double door leading from the winery to the barrel room. The Gothic-style, solid oak door was constructed by the Peples using handmade nails, each with a dogwood motif on the head. The same blacksmith who struck the nails also created the wrought-iron hinges. The bare bones of an old corncrib have been incorporated and fleshed out to create the retail area, offset slightly from the new construction.

Grayhaven currently specializes in dry white wines. Their *Fumé Blanc* is a 100 percent Sauvignon Blanc with a light touch of toasted oak and a growing, lingering finish. Their only red wine, a Maréchal Foch varietal, is a dry wine as well, but they take a tentative leap off the all-dry wagon

The name of Lyn and Charles's winery comes from J. R. R. Tolkien's *Ring* trilogy. In this epic fantasy Grayhavens is an area bordering the sea where you can lead a quiet, peaceful, and successful life. The challenges they faced in starting and growing their business soon proved to the Peples that winegrowing is no fairy tale. It is, on the other hand, an occupation which allows those with "energy, ingenuity, and creativity" to produce something useful and beautiful which others can in turn enjoy and appreciate. Life really doesn't offer anything better than that.

with their Riesling, an Alsatian-style sipping wine with a mere 1 percent residual sugar. Plans are to start using more Cayuga in their blends and save the Seyval for making a sparkling wine—*méthode champenoise* of course.

Grayhaven is open on Saturdays and Sundays. At other times you should call ahead to make sure someone will be at the winery. If you just show up, you may find everyone in the vineyards. If it's early August, you may be asked to help throw netting. Several miles of net are unrolled and draped over their vines each year to protect the ripening fruit from one of a winegrower's most dreaded apparitions—a sky dark and shrill with crows, or any of their grape-devouring cousins.

If you prefer less strenuous work, up at the winery Lyn has been known to let customers participate in the winemaking experience by "dressing" a bottle of wine—applying the label and the capsule by hand.

The hiking trail through the woods at Grayhaven follows an old dirt road that winds with laborious expediency among old trees. Shade-seeking wild flowers reward the sharp-eyed, and the careful observer will eventually spot *Vitis riparia*, or river vine, growing not far from the creek. The wild, native grapevine bears its small berries high up in the branches of its host tree—easy pickings for the crow but not for the fox, who tends to label them sour anyway.

HILL TOP BERRY FARM

Hill Top Berry Farm and Winery
2800 Berry Hill Road
Nellysford, VA 22958

Hours: 11 a.m. to 5 p.m. Wednesday through Sunday. Extended hours during blackberry season (July 4 through September 5): 9 a.m. to 6 p.m. Monday through Saturday and 10 a.m. to 6 p.m. on Sunday. Closed January 15 through April 15, Thanksgiving, Christmas Day, and New Year's Day.

Directions: From **Charlottesville,** take I-64 west to Crozet (exit 107). Go west on Rte. 250, then south on Rte. 151 for approximately 10 miles and turn left onto Rte. 612 at Tuckahoe Antique Mall. Bear right across the bridge. Winery is on the left at the top of the hill.

Phone: 804-361-1266
Fax: 804-361-1266
E-mail: hilltop1@intelos.net

Tasting fee: None

Wines: Fruit Wines, including Blackberry, Raspberry, Plum, Peach, Apple; and *Virginia Blush*

Wine related items for sale? Yes
Picnic area? Yes

Owners: Marlyn and Sue Allen
Winemaker: Marlyn Allen

Blackberries are to be had a number of ways at this winery in Nellysford, just a few miles from the Wintergreen ski resort. From approximately the Fourth of July until the first week in September, visitors to Hill Top Berry Farm are invited to pick their own. There are six acres of blackberries here, with eight different varieties ripening continuously over a two-month period. According to owner Marlyn Allen, an experienced customer can fill a gallon container with berries from his thorn-free vines in just ten minutes.

Blackberries need insects, especially bees, for pollination, but there are not enough wild bees roaming the farm to keep six densely planted acres pollinated, so each spring Marlyn and wife Sue rely on contract labor, renting several hives from a local beekeeper. The honey is sold at the winery. "We keep the bees on the blackberry blossoms," says Marlyn, "and it's the closest thing to blackberry blossom honey that you're going to get."

The Allens also make wine that's as close to blackberry heaven as you're likely to get in this life, and they offer it in three versions. Marlyn's dry (silver cap) and semi-dry (gold cap) renditions are clear, garnet-colored, tannicly passive alternatives to serve with many dishes you might otherwise accompany with a light, Beaujolais-style red. For those who can't contemplate a fruit wine that isn't at least a little bit sweet, Hill Top's *Blackberry Delight* is a dessert wine with something in the neighborhood of 3 percent residual sugar.

Blackberries grow in profuse disarray in the wild or in a back corner of your suburban lot. But on the Allens' farm they are neatly trellised, and the initial impression when you arrive at the winery is that these are grapevines. They have other things in common with wine grapes as well. Once the blackberry vines are established, they become very dry-weather tolerant. If they are not irrigated at the start, they will send their roots deep into the earth the way grapevines do. Like grapes, they don't like a lot of rain once they begin to ripen. Mold and mildew are seldom a problem for the Allens because their vines are planted on hills. Drainage is good, and water sources in the valleys—a man-made pond and several springs—keep the air circulating in the berry fields. Like grapevines, blackberries have to be pruned back every winter.

Hill Top is carving out its niche with specialty wines. They have planted small blocks of Concord and Niagara grapes—two American varieties—but so far there are no vinifera or French hybrids here. They've also planted plum trees and peach trees and will be making these fruit wines in the future. At present, besides blackberry, they're producing a slightly sweet raspberry and a dry apple wine. They also made their first boysenberry wine and Concord grape wine in 1999 and will be experimenting with currants, gooseberries, and mulberries.

Grapes and berry vines do quite well in arid surroundings, but mushrooms like it better where it's not so hot and dry. The shiitakes the Allens grow are happier down in the hollows where the springs create a cooler, damper microclimate. Marlyn inoculates white oak logs with the shiitake spores, and in six to eight months a seemingly uncultivatable portion of his farm is blooming with the edible fungus. You can't pick your own mushrooms or buy them at the winery, but occasionally Marlyn, who likes to diversify on a small scale, has a little ginseng root and goldenseal for sale.

The Allens harvest the big, luscious, midnight purple blackberries by hand, crush them by hand, and press them by hand. They even hand-carry the juice in buckets up three flights of stairs to the fermentation vats in their new winery. From there things get a little easier as the process flows naturally from one level to the next. Hands take over again when it's time for bottling, corking, and labeling. The winery was built from the foundation up by the Allens, with considerable help from family members and friends in the berry business. The solid walnut bar with birch base was handcrafted by colleagues eager to help get the winery up and running.

When Marlyn decided he might want to start making mead, he turned to a fellow winery owner, who freely shared his knowledge and experience on the subject. Before too long the Allens may be making something that comes as close as you're going to get to a blackberry blossom honey-mead wine—just one more way for visitors to enjoy blackberries at Hill Top Berry Farm.

Horton Cellars Winery

Horton Cellars Winery
6399 Spotswood Trail
Gordonsville, VA 22942

Hours: 10 a.m. to 5 p.m. daily, except Thanksgiving, Christmas Day, and New Year's Day. Call ahead for in-depth tours.

Directions: From **Richmond,** take I-64 west to Rte. 15 north to Gordonsville circle. Cross circle and take Rte. 33 west for 4 miles. Winery is on the right. From **Charlottesville,** take Rte. 29 north, or from **DC** (via I-66 west) take Rte. 29 south to Ruckersville, then Rte. 33 east for 8 miles to winery on left. From I-95 at **Fredericksburg,** take Rte. 3 west to Rte. 20 south to Orange, then Rte. 15 south to Gordonsville circle, then Rte. 33 west for 4 miles to winery on the right.

Phone: 540-832-7440
Fax: 540-832-7187
E-mail: vawinee@aol.com
Website: www.hvwine.com

Tasting fee: None

Wines: Chardonnay, Viognier, Cabernet Franc, Marsanne, Vidal Blanc, Syrah, Mourvedre, Touriga Nacional, Rkatsiteli, Norton, vintage port, fruit wines

Wine related items for sale? Yes
Picnic area? Yes
Food available? Light snacks
Facilities for private functions? Yes

Owners: Dennis Horton, Joan Bieda
Winemaker: Graham Bell
Viticulturist: Sharon Horton

The story goes that it was a walk in the woods that led to the rediscovery of the Norton grape. It was at first thought to be a patch of native wild, or fox, grapes—until someone noticed that the vines were all arranged in rows and that these were spaced equal distances apart. The vineyard had in all likelihood been abandoned during Prohibition. Over the years the forest had slowly crept up on it and surrounded it, but it continued to bear fruit, hidden away, until its appointed hour, in its sylvan setting.

The Norton is a true Virginia variety, a hybrid attributed to a certain Dr. Norton of Richmond. The complete details of its origins, including its precise parentage, are difficult to verify, as is the tale of how the remnants of this grape—once thought to be entirely extinct—were found. One thing is without question: it was Dennis Horton who planted the first modern Norton vines in Virginia, and his winery produced the first Norton wine in the state since Prohibition. Interestingly, the surviving grapes were not found in Virginia but in Missouri, where both Dennis and Sharon Horton grew up. Another undisputed fact is the growing popularity of this variety, which at the turn of the century was the premier grape of the Virginia wine industry. Horton Cellars bottles over 4,000 cases of a Norton varietal each year, and it outsells every other wine they make two to one.

Dennis is one of those people who never seem to jump on a bandwagon. Instead he builds them. The first grape he planted at Horton Vineyards, in 1989, was a little-known Rhone variety called Viognier. Only two years later, in part because they helped the young vines along with irrigation, the Hortons harvested a small crop. Winemaker Graham Bell recalls that 1993 was a very dry year in Virginia, resulting in a low yield from the now maturing vines that produced an extremely good wine. It was an immediate success, winning awards in California and garnering the start-up winery much press nationwide. Viognier is now showing up on more and more wine lists across Virginia and the rest of the country.

Another first for Horton came in 1995 when they produced the first port to be made in Virginia since the Eighteenth Amendment was revoked. They originally used the stalwart Norton as the base, although they now also make it, appropriately, from two Portuguese varieties they have subsequently planted, Touriga Nacional and Tinta Cão. Port is a very sweet after dinner wine, having about 5 to 6 percent residual sugar, and is fortified with spirits that bring its alcohol level up to around 18 percent. At Horton they ferment this traditional Portuguese wine in open vats. When the sugar level is just right, they add 150 proof distilled alcohol, which slows the fermentation drastically.

When they initially decided to try their hand at making port, the winery encountered an arcane statute that required vintners to themselves produce the spirits that go into the wine rather than buy them. When he looked into what would be involved, Dennis Horton quickly came to the conclusion that it would be easier to change the law than try to comply with all its attendant regulations. He persuaded Virginia's lawmakers to get rid of an archaic and counterproductive piece of legislation—much as Congress did when it decided to undo Prohibition, proving that some laws are made to be repealed.

Horton is one of Virginia's largest wineries, producing most of its annual 35,000 cases from 100 acres divided among four different sites it either owns or leases. Sharon Horton manages the vineyards. Her background in nursing is reflected in the pristine conditions to be found at all four locations. The two largest vineyards are just outside the town

of Orange, approximately ten miles from the winery. There are also several acres at the Hortons' home in nearby Madison County. The smallest vineyard is the one at the winery. Here the land is low lying and not ideal for most grapes, according to Graham. The five acres of Russian Rkatsiteli do well here, however. As you approach the winery from Gordonsville, the vines on your right present the image of a petite château in a continuum of impressions snatched from between the rows—as if you were glimpsing it through the riffled slats of vertical blinds.

Dennis Horton designed the basic architecture, which combines English half timber with lots of stonework. The interior spaces are big and airy. There's a second story, multipurpose gathering room with french windows that look out over a beautifully appointed tasting room and gift shop. Access to the winery proper is via the turret, and the echoing clang of your steps on the circular stairway adds to the sensation that you're descending into the nether regions of a small castle. At the landing you get a panoramic view of the production area. Huge stainless steel tanks and gigantic oak vats occupy the center of the underground chamber with its insulating stone walls. Off to the left are four deep, dark bays where oak barrels range from floor to ceiling in cool, cave-like conditions.

In a given year Horton Cellars produces about thirty different wines, including five or six fruit wines in their *Château Le Cabin* series. In addition to the more traditional Chardonnays, Vidals, and Bordeaux reds, Graham Bell is making varietals and blends from some interesting but less familiar grapes. Dennis seems to favor the Rhone Valley varieties, mainly because the summers in this region of southern France are almost as hot as the summers in Virginia. Besides Viognier—Mourvedre, Marsanne, Syrah, and Grenache appear frequently on the list. There's an extraordinary grape called Tannat (the name surely means pure tannin), which Graham uses to add structure to his Cabernet Franc. And of course that incredible comeback grape, the Norton.

All tastings at wineries involve a discussion of wine and food pairings, which eventually leads to some back and forth about what goes best with chocolate desserts. The Bordeaux reds are often mentioned because of their cherry and raspberry overtones. This prompted one taster to suggest to Graham that his sweet, slightly tart raspberry wine might be a suitable accompaniment, to which Horton's winemaker drolly countered that "milk and chocolate go together pretty well." It's recommended that you chill the milk several hours before serving.

Horton Cellars Winery

JEFFERSON VINEYARDS

Jefferson Vineyards
1353 Thomas Jefferson Pkwy.
Charlottesville, VA 22902

Hours: 11 a.m. to 5 p.m. daily, except Thanksgiving, Christmas Day, and New Year's Day. Tours conducted on the hour from noon until 4 p.m.

Directions: From **I-64**, take exit 121A toward Scottsville. Immediately past the light, turn left onto Hwy 53 and go 3 miles to the winery entrance, on the right.

Phone: 804-977-3042
Fax: 804-977-5459
E-mail: info@jeffersonvineyards.com
Website: www.jeffersonvineyards.com

Tasting fee: None

Wines: Chardonnay, Pinot Gris, Riesling, Cabernet Sauvignon, Cabernet Franc, Merlot, *Meritage, Estate Reserve, Capriccio*

Wine related items for sale? Yes
Picnic area? Yes
Food available? Light snacks
Special Programs? Case Club
Facilities for private functions? Yes

Owners: the Woodward family
Winemaker: Michael Shaps
Viticulturist: Chris Hill

After the harvest of color is over and the wind has gleaned the last bit of scarlet, purple, and gold from the trees, visitors can get a glimpse of these vineyards from Monticello, Thomas Jefferson's mountaintop home in Charlottesville.

In 1773, convinced that wines on a par with Europe's finest could be produced in Virginia, Jefferson gave the land now occupied by the winery to Filippo Mazzei. In 1774, with the help of vignerons from his own country, the Italian viticulturist—who had been recommended by none other than Benjamin Franklin—planted vinifera varieties in soils adjacent to the original Monticello tract. But the fledgling enterprise was interrupted in 1778 when Mazzei gave up raising grapes and returned to Europe to raise money for the cause of American independence. During the Revolution, Hessian mercenaries, prisoners of war quartered on the property, went carousing through the vineyards on horseback, trampling the tender young vines. Not a trace of the vineyards remains today.

What does remain is the foundation of the house that Mazzei built. Christened Colle—Italian for "mountain pass"—the original structure was torn down sometime in the 1930s and its timbers and dormer windows used in the reconstruction of historic Michie Tavern, less than a mile down the road. A new Colle was erected in 1940, on Mazzei's foundation, by the present owners of the winery. In 1939 the Woodward family acquired the 650-acre parcel known as Simeon Farm. In 1981 Stanley Woodward, Sr. planted new vines—all vinifera—and five years later the winery opened its doors as Simeon Vineyards. For the first few years the business was run more or less as a pastime. Woodward's son, Stanley, Jr., believing the operation could be turned into a viable commercial enterprise, later decided to call it Jefferson Vineyards, an appellation with slightly more name recognition.

In 1995 the Woodwards hired Michael Shaps as winemaker. In less than two years the graduate of the Lycée Viticole de Beaune in France brought annual production at the winery from 4,000 cases to its current 8,000. True to his *lycée*, Michael embraces the philosophy and techniques taught at the Burgundian school of winemaking. Its first principal is an often cited one: wine is made in the vineyard. To help him here he relies on local viticultural legend Chris Hill to manage the twenty on-site acres and thirty additional land-lease acres at various locations around Charlottesville. According to Michael, Virginia's climate is very similar to that of Bordeaux, which experiences the same generally humid conditions, as well as the all too frequent problem of heavy rains during harvest. "Chris has developed his own methods for dealing with the challenging Virginia climate. He always brings me excellent fruit," Michael says, "even in the tough years." A few minutes at the tasting bar is all the proof

you need that Michael is turning this same fruit into some truly excellent wines.

Inside the winery French methods translate to minimal manipulation of the wine. More often than not, Michael's wines, especially the Bordeaux varietals and blends, are fined with egg whites rather than filtered. This stabilizes the wines without robbing them of any of the flavor nuances that contribute to their complexity. Whole-berry, or whole-cluster, pressing is another Burgundian technique sometimes used at Jefferson, as is the use of native yeast for fermenting one of their Chardonnays, a wine they call *Fantaisie Sauvage*—with a nod to the wild yeast naturally present on the skins of all grapes. An inveterate experimenter, Michael segregates the grapes at crush in order to assess the effects of the highly mutable yeasts indigenous to each vineyard. For the reserve Chardonnay the winemaker uses yeast imported from France and puts the wine up in bottles made in France as well. They are fashioned after a bottle of 1787 Château Lafite found in a cellar in Paris and bearing what are presumed to be Thomas Jefferson's initials. Jefferson was ambassador to France at the time, and the bottle may well be an example of eighteenth-century private-labeling.

A former stable houses the winery's hospitality room, where it's standing room only. There's plenty of seating out on the deck, however. Bring a picnic lunch if you like. Or pick up something at BRIX Marketplace. This hamlet-sized restaurant and delicatessen across the road from the winery offers gourmet selections just made to pair with one of Jefferson's superb wines. The tasting room's shaded deck is within paper airplane range of the winery proper. On a warm afternoon in mid October, the piquant aroma from an open fermentation tub set outside on the crush pad may draw you out of your chair and across the gravel driveway. An intern, a graduate of one of the winemaking schools in Bordeaux or Dijon, may be busy punching down the cap on a sampler vat of Petit Verdot, Tannat, or another of Michael's experimental varieties. Parlez-vous francais?—or German, Hungarian, or Czech? Does he speak English? Your reciprocal levels of fluency will determine the extent of the exchange, which may be limited to a smile and a nod, accompanied by the soft, rhythmic gurgle of grape skins going under.

Despite his own personal disappointments, Thomas Jefferson continued in his belief that one day his lands, and Virginia as a whole, would produce wines to compare to the best that Europe had to offer. Thanks to winemaker Michael Shaps, today, at the foot of his beloved Monticello, this namesake winery is doing Mr. Jefferson proud.

Mountain Cove Vineyards

Mountain Cove Vineyards
and Winegarden
1362 Fortunes Cove Lane
Lovingston, VA 22949

Hours: Noon to 6 p.m. Wednesday through Sunday and on federal holiday Mondays. Open by appointment only in January. Closed Thanksgiving and Christmas Day.

Directions: From **Lovingston**, take Rte. 29 north and turn left onto Rte. 718 (Mountain Cove Road), then right onto Rte. 651. Winery is on the right, 3.5 miles from Rte. 29. From **Richmond** (via I-64) and **Charlottesville**, take Rte. 29 south towards Lovingston. Turn right onto Rte. 718 and follow directions above.

Phone: 800-489-5392
804-263-5392
Fax: 804-263-8540
E-mail: aweed1@juno.com

Tasting fee: None, except $3 per person for groups of over 20 (Includes souvenir glass.)

Wines: Chardonnay, blended reds and whites, fruit wines, and *Fortunes Cove Ginseng Gold* herbal wine

Wine related items for sale? Yes
Picnic area? Yes
Facilities for private functions? Yes

Owners: A. C. (Al) and Emily Weed
Winemaker/Viticulturist: Al Weed

A cove is an inlet in a shoreline that can provide safe haven and shelter from a storm. A mountain cove is a hollow among the hills, and if it also has a rustic farm winery, it's a perfect haven to turn into to escape the madly rushing currents of modern living. Al Weed is the owner of Mountain Cove Vineyards, and an escape from the hectic pace of Washington, D.C., was what he had in mind when he relocated his family to sixty acres on the eastern slopes of the Blue Ridge Mountains.

An alumnus of Yale and Princeton, Al was working as an investment banker when he finally heeded the calling he'd had since boyhood to own and operate a farm. It was 1973, and there were at most two or three vineyards in the whole state of Virginia when Al decided to give up banking and become a grape farmer. He had visited all four of Maryland's wineries and figured he could do just as well growing French hybrids here. The ones he chose were Baco Noir, Cascade, Chancellor, and Chelois—all reds—and Villard Blanc.

Al was a young winegrower in his thirties when he helped Archie Smith, Jr. of Meredyth Vineyards draft a bill that became the 1980 Virginia Farm Wineries Act. The importance of this legislation in establishing a political climate in which the state's reemerging wine industry could grow and prosper cannot be overstated, and Al was one of the industry's earliest pioneers.

In 1997, twenty years after making his first wine, Al realized it was time not only for retrellising but also for regrouping. In the years since he had planted his hybrids, enormous progress had been made in Virginia in the growing of wine grapes, particularly the European varieties. Al tore out 90 percent of his existing vines—everything but the Villard Blanc—and replanted in a mix of vinifera (Cabernet Sauvignon, Cabernet Franc), French hybrid (Chambourcin), and the increasingly popular Norton, a Virginia hybrid. While he waits for his new vines to mature, he makes his wine from grapes bought on the open market and from his original Villard Blanc. Says Al, "We're basically starting all over." In a quirky way, one of the oldest wineries in Virginia is in the process of becoming one of its newest.

In selecting the new varieties for his vineyard, Al was looking for several things. First, they had to have names that people recognized. His original four reds are all widely grown in France. But even there, he admits, they're used mainly for blending, and the names are seldom on the label.

Equally important, Al wanted grapes that would ripen late in the season. His earlier hybrids ripened in late August or early September. He had to pick them as soon as they were ripe. Otherwise, in the hot, humid, and often very rainy weeks that followed here in Virginia, the grapes—which were very vulnerable to fungus—would rot in front of his eyes. "Through all the work that had been done at Virginia Tech," Al explains, "especially the research of state enologist Bruce Zoecklein, it had become apparent that it's important to let the fruit hang on the vine for a while after it's notionally ripe." Hanging allows the character of the variety to fully develop and also reduces the level of tannins. "What aging in oak barrels does," he adds, "is to soften the tannins. If you can soften the tannins on the vine, you can make a wine that has all of the complexities and all of the desirability that an aged red wine has, but you can release it much sooner." His new reds will ripen in mid to late September—the Norton as late as November—and can hang for several weeks after that.

"What we're trying to do at Mountain Cove," says Al, "is to create a destination." The problem is that once you get here you just don't want to leave. When you step inside the tasting room, you're surrounded with the homeyness of a little country store. Wine bottles are neatly displayed in wooden vegetable bins and there's a large selection of home-style

Central Region

34

dainties from Vidalia onion honey mustard dressing to damson plum preserves. After the complimentary wine tasting, you can mosey outside and sit for a while on the front porch or find a spot on the lawn to soak up the sun and the scenery. If it gets a little warm, slip around the retaining wall to the grape arbor and hang out with the Cayuga and Villard Blanc under a cool, leafy canopy. There's a large pavilion that looks out over Al's new vineyard where you can have a picnic lunch.

Although it's only about twenty years old, the winery has a definite vintage look. It's built into the side of a hill and provides great natural insulation for the barrels and case goods, helped by the stone facing on the sixteen-inch walls. Where did all those stones come from? "Right out of the creek down here," says Al, with a wave of his arm in a direction you won't find on your compass.

For those who may find the average Cabernet Sauvignon a little too tannic, Mountain Cove makes a nonconfrontational, 100 percent varietal that Al calls *Tinto Virginia*. It's a Spanish-style red that gets only two days of skin contact, so it's light and refreshing, with little tannin. He's also making a delightful wine out of Villard Blanc and five locally grown herbs, including ginseng, ginger, anise, hyssop, and lemon balm, and the label reminds you that "the tonic properties of these herbs have been recognized for centuries." You will certainly start to feel better after a sip or two. So good, in fact, you'll probably want to buy a bottle and head for the pavilion.

A slowly unwinding afternoon in a hidden valley away from the hustle and bustle of everywhere else, and in your hand a glass of Mountain Cove's herbal wine. It's good for what ails you.

Oakencroft Vineyard and Winery

Oakencroft Vineyard and Winery
1486 Oakencroft Lane
Charlottesville, VA 22901

Hours: 11 a.m. to 5 p.m. daily April through December; 11 a.m. to 5 p.m. on weekends in March; by appointment during January and February. Closed Easter, Thanksgiving, and Christmas Day.

Directions: From **Rte. 29,** go 3.5 miles west on Rte. 654 (Barracks Road, which becomes Garth Road). Entrance is on the left. From **Richmond,** take I-64 west to exit 118B onto 250/29 Bypass. At Rte. 654 (Barracks Road) turn left and follow signs to winery. From **D.C.,** take I-66 west to Rte. 29 south. Turn right at exit for I-64/Staunton/Lynchburg. Take Barracks Road exit and turn right at the light. Go 3 miles to winery, on the right.

Phone: 804-296-4188
Fax: 804-293-6631
E-mail: fwr@oakencroft.com
Website: www.oakencroft.com

Tasting fee: $1 per person ($3 per person for tasting and souvenir glass)

Wines: Cabernet Sauvignon, Cabernet Franc, Chardonnay, Merlot, *Countryside Red, Countryside White, Sweet Virginia*

Wine related items for sale? Yes
Picnic area? Yes
Facilities for private functions? Yes

Owner: Felicia Warburg Rogan
Winemaker: Michael Shaps
Viticulturist: Philip Ponton

Drive slowly after you enter the gates at Oakencroft and be alert, because at this winery the geese have the right of way. Wild waterfowl often take to the lake in front of the winery in great numbers. It's not unusual for one or more to suddenly waddle up the embankment and cross the road—without looking either way—to have a gander at what's on the other side.

The lake in front of Oakencroft's tasting room is long and narrow, like the winery complex itself. On a still, clear day it presents a perfect mirror image of the red frame building with its broad, stone-facade entrance. Adirondack chairs at water's edge invite you to assume a sedentary attitude while sipping one of the award-winning wines produced at this midsized winery, the oldest currently operating winemaking establishment in Albemarle County and the closest one to Charlottesville.

Felicia Warburg Rogan grew up in New York City where she learned to appreciate fine wines at an early age. When she married her late husband, John Rogan, in 1977 and moved to his 250-acre cattle farm in central Virginia, she discovered that the local culture did not consider wine to be *de rigueur* as part of a meal, even a great one, and it was next to impossible to get a glass of white wine at a cocktail party. Virginia was just rediscovering its grape growing past, however, and Felicia, at the urging of a friend, visited one of the state's new vineyards on the Northern Neck. It was during crush, and Felicia and John were able to pick some grapes and bring home some of the newly pressed juice. They made their first batch of "garage wine" that year. "It was terrible," admits Felicia, "but it was fun." It also made the suggestion of a small, experimental vineyard next to the house seem like a good idea.

After subsequent homemade vintages began to win amateur awards, Felicia thought she might like to start her own winery. In 1982 she hired a consulting viticulturist to select a more suitable vineyard site on the property and planted seventeen acres in Chardonnay, Cabernet Sauvignon, Merlot, and Seyval Blanc. Oakencroft received its farm winery license the following year. With the help of her husband, a real estate developer and owner of the Boar's Head Inn in Charlottesville, the current production and retail facility was constructed, using an old cowshed as the nucleus of the elongated building.

Susceptibility to frost in some parts of the vineyard has reduced the acreage at the farm from seventeen to its current twelve, so Felicia supplements with grapes from other Virginia vineyards in order to meet the requirements of the winery's 6,500-case annual production. Vineyardist Philip Ponton has been with Oakencroft from its inception and gets the credit for the exceptional quality of the fruit being produced here. Consulting winemaker Michael Shaps (Jefferson Vineyards) has responsibility for turning Philip's grapes into award winning wines, a duty he can be expected to perform with predictable regularity.

Oakencroft's list includes vinifera varietals—Chardonnay, Merlot, Cabernet Sauvignon—and several proprietary blends. *Countryside White* is a mix of French hybrid varieties with only a hint of sweetness, while its counterpart, *Countryside Red,* retains 2 percent residual sugar in a hybrid and vinifera blend. The wines can be sampled in the tasting room as part of the standard wine review. Wine jellies made from Oakencroft's Chambourcin-based blush and their Merlot can be enjoyed with a picnic lunch at tables in the courtyard looking out towards the lake.

Few people have been as active in nurturing the growth of the renascent Virginia wine industry as Felicia Warburg Rogan. In 1981, shortly after planting her own commercial

vines, she organized a group of vineyard owners in the Charlottesville area into the Jeffersonian Wine Grape Growers Society. Under the auspices of the association, a museum to house wine-related artifacts and tell the story of winemaking in Virginia was established at historic Michie Tavern, less than a mile from Thomas Jefferson's home at Monticello. The designation of the enormously productive grape growing region around Charlottesville as the Monticello viticultural appellation was also accomplished through the efforts of the Society under Felicia's leadership.

In 1985 Felicia was appointed to and elected first chairman of the newly chartered Virginia Winegrowers Advisory Board, a body created by the state's general assembly to offer assistance and promotion to Virginia's young and rapidly growing wine industry. Felicia has served as a member and chair of the board during numerous subsequent terms. Love for the art of winegrowing led to the publication in 1987 of her book, *Virginia Wines: A Vineyard Year,* a history of viticulture in the state and the winemaking process. She has taken her personal commitment to promoting Virginia wines beyond the borders of the commonwealth and even the country, having travelled to France and Japan on trade-related missions with two governors.

It's unlikely that Felicia Rogan realized when she planted her experimental vines next to the house that she would play such an important role in the successful progress of winemaking in Virginia. Now dedicated to promoting the wines of the Monticello appellation, she sums up the decades-long experience with this modest observation: "It's been fun watching this industry grow and being a part of it."

Prince Michel de Virginia

Prince Michel de Virginia and Rapidan River Vineyards
HCR4, Box 77
South Route 29
Leon, VA 22725

Hours: 10 a.m. to 5 p.m. daily, except Thanksgiving, Christmas, and New Year's Day.

Directions: Located on the west side of Rte. 29. From **Culpeper**, take Rte. 29 south for 9 miles. From **Charlottesville**, take Rte. 29 north for 30 miles. From **Richmond**, take I-64 west to Charlottesville, then take Rte. 29 north for 30 miles.

Phone: 540-547-3707
Fax: 540-547-3088
E-mail: info@princemichel.com
Website: www.princemichel.com

Tasting fee: $2 per person

Wines: Cabernet Sauvignon, Merlot, Merlot-Cabernet blend, Chardonnay, Riesling, Gewürztraminer, *Sweet Reserve*, brut sparkling wine

Wine related items for sale? Yes
Food available? Full service restaurant
Special Programs? Wine Club
Facilities for private functions? Yes

Owner: Jean Leducq
Winemaker: Tom Payette

If you want to learn a lot about winemaking in a short time, start your pilgrimage to the Virginia wineries here. None does a better job of educating visitors about the ancient art and modern science of viniculture than Prince Michel.

The climates and soils of Virginia are often compared to those of the famous winegrowing regions of France, and it is not only Virginia winemakers who are of the opinion that wines equal to those of Gallic origin can be and, in fact, already are being produced in the Old Dominion. It's significant, then, that when Jean Leducq finally fulfilled his lifelong dream of owning a winery, he did so near the small town of Leon in the foothills of the Blue Ridge Mountains. Since establishing his vineyards in 1982, the French businessman has been inducted into the prestigious Order of la Jurade, a fraternity founded in England nearly 800 years ago to honor outstanding achievement in winegrowing and winemaking.

The museum at Prince Michel is Jean Leducq's way of sharing his passion for wine and its history. Most of the things you'll see here were acquired in France and comprise an impressive collection of wine-related artifacts.

There's an interesting display offering a thumbnail biography of Dom Pérignon, cellar master and administrator at the Abbey de Hautvillers in the Champagne region of France. Tradition holds that the venerable seventeenth-century Benedictine monk not only blessed wine lovers forever with the invention of champagne, he also pioneered the development of the cork as the preferred method of sealing a bottle of *vin,* borrowing the idea from pilgrims to his abbey. A separate display explains in detail the process whereby the spongy bark of the cork oak tree is elevated to the noble station of being entrusted with the sometimes decades-long preservation of the world's finest wines.

Among the hundreds of artifacts on display are an array of grape harvesting baskets—precursors of the modern-day yellow plastic lug; a case containing antique pruning and harvesting implements; and a collection of corkscrews ranging from the very primitive to ornate silver- and brass-handle versions of the most revered of all bottle openers. Examples of machinery and equipment from earlier periods chronicle the evolution of vineyard maintenance and grape processing.

Prince Michel is named, in part, for a friend of Jean Leducq's, the son of the exiled king of Poland. Before leaving the museum, take a minute to read the wall panel that pays homage to historical personages of the same name who have played a role in the promotion and advancement of winemaking throughout the centuries.

From the museum, the self-guided tour proceeds along a gallery overlooking the production area. Winemaker Tom Payette remembers when there were only a few tanks and perhaps twenty oak barrels in here. Now the oak has been crowded out to make room for close to two dozen stainless steel tanks. Catwalks between the rows provide cellar workers with intriguing aerial views into the tall, slender vessels. An empty tank does indeed look, as Tom describes it, like a missile silo. At other times, foaming, bubbling, fermenting juice creates a heady commotion close to the rim. Later on, wine that is being pumped out leaves the tank in a colorful, swirling vortex.

Cold filtration to remove harmless tartrate crystals is standard practice at most Virginia wineries. The tanks used for this purpose at Prince Michel can be warmed up as well as cooled down, which expedites the bottling process. As Tom explains, measurable change occurs in the volume of a liquid like wine as the temperature rises or falls. A wine bottled at between sixty-two and sixty-five degrees Fahrenheit has considerably more room for expansion than would one put up at a chilly thirty-five degrees.

The cork is an inextricable part—sometimes quite literally—of the mystique and the enjoyment of wine. The little bit of trouble we have to go to in order to open a bottle only serves to enhance our appreciation of its contents. In its simplicity the cork is a thing of beauty in both form and function. It works by filling the neck of the bottle so tightly that virtually no air can get in to oxidize and degrade the wine. Modern equipment employs several methods to ensure that oxygen in the bottle is all but completely eliminated. At Prince Michel, a burst of heavier-than-air nitrogen not only removes any dust particles that may be in the bottles, it also replaces the oxygen. Further down the line, after the bottles have been filled, a jaw-like device compresses the cork. Just before the cork is inserted, the machine plays it safe by pulling a quick vacuum on the bottle.

From the winery your bird's eye tour continues into the barrel room. French and American oak vessels stacked three and four high rise to meet you as you stroll along the balcony that traverses the quiet, dimly lit wine-aging chamber below. High up, on an outcrop in the wall, an on-premises cooper is busy assembling another barrel. The lifelike mannequin is undistracted by your presence as he stands quietly at his task. Tom Payette generally approves of the cooper's work, commenting that "he moves very slow, but he's consistent day in and day out."

Stationed along the gallery on the tour are a number of lighted dioramas. They provide succinct yet explicit accounts of different aspects of grape growing and winemaking. There's a display dealing with the various stages the vines go through as the seasons progress. You'll learn that after the vines have been sharply pruned back in January, the graft unions—where European vines have been joined to the hardier, more disease-resistant American rootstock—are covered over with topsoil to protect them during the often bitter cold winter months in Virginia.

In other dioramas you'll see how mechanical harvesters gently shake the individual ripe grapes from the vines. Hand-harvested clusters, on the other hand, go into destemmers, which use centrifugal force to whirl the loosely attached berries from their stems. The different paths that red and white grapes take from vine to wine are illustrated in displays entitled "Crushing and Pressing" and "Fermentation." White grapes are usually fermented at cool temperatures, around fifty-five degrees Fahrenheit, to preserve their fruity characteristics. Vat temperatures for red grapes normally hover around eighty-five degrees, to aid in the extraction of color from the skins.

There are approximately 100 acres of grapes in production in Leon, where the winery is located. Prince Michel also owns Rapidan River Vineyards in nearby Culpeper. From these and other vineyards it leases or owns, the winery is producing 35,000 cases a year. The wine list is broken out by vineyard. The Chardonnays come from the Prince Michel vineyard, as do the Cabernet Sauvignon and Merlot varietals. Rapidan River provides the grapes for a Pinot Noir varietal and two Rieslings—a semi-dry and a dry, Alsatian-style. Tom Payette is also creating a limited-edition series that includes a Rapidan River Gewürztraminer and a brut sparkling wine appropriately designated as *The Prince's.*

Prince Michel de Virginia

The four-diamond Prince Michel Restaurant offers prix-fixe lunch and dinner menus Thursday through Saturday, as well as lunch on Sunday. The authentic French cuisine is prepared by Master Chef Alain Lecomte, who used to cook for Jean Leducq's company in France. The restaurant's hours coincide with the extended weekend schedule of the Suites at Prince Michel. In *La Concorde, Les Champs Élysées, La Tour Eiffel,* or the *Paris* suite, visitors can overnight in country French luxury in a very private setting overlooking the vineyards.

There's a wonderful romantic aura about wine and winemaking, but as Tom Payette points out, "a lot of work goes into creating romance." The French Provincial mood of the architecture, the elegant ambience of the restaurant, the wines themselves, and even the name: Prince Michel—at this winery no effort has been spared to entangle you in an *affaire de cœur* with the vine.

41

Rebec Vineyards

Rebec Vineyards
2229 North Amherst Highway
Amherst, VA 24521

Hours: 10 a.m. to 5 p.m. daily.

Directions: Located on the west side of Rte. 29 between Lynchburg and Charlottesville, 5 miles north of Amherst and 11 miles south of Lovingston. From **northern Virginia** and **D.C.**, take I-66 to Rte. 29 south. From **Winchester** and **Harrisonburg,** take I-81 south to I-64 east to Rte. 29 south. From **Richmond,** take I-64 west to Rte. 29 south at Charlottesville. From the **Roanoke area,** take Rte. 460 east to **Lynchburg,** then Rte. 29 north.

Phone: 804-946-5168

Tasting fee: None, except $2 per person for groups of 10 or more

Wines: Cabernet Sauvignon, Merlot, Pinot Noir, Viognier, Chardonnay, Gewürztraminer, Riesling, *Autumn Glow, Sweet Sofia, Landmark White, Sweetbriar Rose*

Wine related items for sale? Yes
Special Programs? Annual Garlic Festival

Owner: Richard Hanson
Winemaker: Svetlozar Kanev

The two-story white house at Mountain View Farm is more than 250 years old. There are no nails in the lap-siding structure; wooden pegs hold this colonial-era dwelling together. In 1831 it was completely dismantled and moved from its original location seventeen miles away and reassembled, board by board, at its current site in Amherst County.

Ella Hanson's grandmother moved here as a young bride in the 1880s and planted a rosebush next to the front porch. Over a century later the pink floribunda, now a sprawling shrub that dominates its side of the house, is covered all spring and summer with delicately tinted blossoms. The house simultaneously celebrated its designation as a Virginia Historic Landmark and National Historic Place in 1999. Surrounding it are the original smokehouse, the icehouse, and a catalog of other outbuildings, or "ordinaries," necessary to the operation of a self-sufficient nineteenth-century Virginia farm. The one-room office behind the house belonged to former owner Dr. Paul Cabell, Amherst County's first resident physician.

Before the blight that struck America's forests in the 1920s decimated their chestnut populations, this hardwood tree was used extensively in construction and furniture making. When the Hansons built their winery in 1980, they recycled the lumber from a 200-year-old tobacco barn on the property. Rare chestnut timbers found their way into the walls and into the tasting room bar. Construction of the winery was strictly a family affair, with Ella's husband, Richard Hanson, and their son-in-law Mark Magruder doing the majority of the work. This small winery, one of the smallest in the state, is also one of the most charming. The slate patina of the beautifully weathered chestnut board-and-batten siding is brightened by red trim, pink roses at the entrance, and the occasional brilliantly decorated salamander skittering across the wooden-plank steps.

Inside, bare wood walls do warm things with the sunlight that enters this small, friendly space through windows with grape-motifed, wrought-iron grilles. We're glad to be here, sampling the vintner's wares, while a tee-shirt on the wall next to the loft balustrade reminds us, in Ben Franklin's words, that "wine is constant proof that God loves us and loves to see us happy."

Ella Hanson was a ballerina and for many years operated a private school of ballet. Like Richard she was a strong supporter of the arts, and Rebec's tasting room is brimming over with the handiwork of local artists and artisans—everything from hand-thrown pottery to hand-turned wooden artifacts. A book of poems written by Ella and her grandson is for sale here also.

If you need something very elegant, there are articles of clothing, tablecloths, and other gifts of hand-worked lace created by the winemaker's relatives in Bulgaria. Besides a ready source of exquisite handmade lace, the former exchange student from Eastern Europe brought with him the recipe for a traditional celebration wine, which the Hansons named *Sweet Sofia* in honor of the capital of Svetlozar Kanev's native country. After fermentation is complete, a portion of the finished white wine is drawn off and at least five different herbs are steeped in the wine to extract their flavors. The herbs are then strained off and the mulled wine is added back to the vat. After sitting for a few days, the wine is bottled. You can make a festive occasion out of attempting to identify the herbs, just sipping the wine, or using it as a marinade for roast chicken à la Rebec.

Svetlozar also makes varietals from Chardonnay, Gewürztraminer, and Riesling. Rebec's dry red is a Cabernet Sauvignon softened with 10 percent Merlot. *Autumn Glow* is a clear, dark rosé, a sweet blend to be enjoyed with dessert—or before dinner while you watch the sun go down, deepening to match the color of the wine.

Minimal physical exertion is required to take the tour at Rebec. It starts in the compact tasting room and proceeds

through a vintage, muntined glass door directly to the compact winery. The stemmer and crusher on the crush pad are two separate pieces of equipment instead of the combination machine other wineries use. They also squeeze their grapes in a manually operated barrel press rather than in the larger, more commonly seen bladder press.

While you're here, you'll learn that before they're bottled, Rebec's wines go through a final cold filtration in a stainless steel refrigeration tank. The temperature is lowered to twenty-three degrees Fahrenheit, which is just below freezing for wine. Solids, including the harmless (but, for some, unappealing) tartrate crystals fall out and collect in the bottom. A quick lesson in bottle sterilization, which includes a high-pressure, superheated wash and a sulfite rinse (for the bottles, not the tourists), usually concludes the brief but informative tour. Back in the tasting room, the easily exhausted can recuperate in a rocking chair before tasting Svetlozar's wines.

Every October this small winery throws one of the biggest parties in Virginia. Over a weekend upwards of 25,000 eager fete-goers gather from around the country and the four corners for the annual Garlic Festival. The wines of Rebec Vineyards and several other local wineries are paired with music, entertainment, and literally scores of dishes prepared with Richard Hanson's favorite condiment, fresh—and only fresh!—garlic.

The rebec was a small, Renaissance instrument resembling a fiddle and in the hands of a skilled musician presumably made some very pleasant music. Rebec Vineyards is a small, renaissance Virginia winery where a skilled winemaker named Svetlozar Kanev is definitely making some very pleasant wines.

ROCKBRIDGE VINEYARD

Rockbridge Vineyard
30 Hill View Lane
Raphine, VA 24472

Hours: 11 a.m. to 5 p.m. Wednesday through Sunday. Closed Thanksgiving Day, December 24, 25, 31, and New Year's Day.

Directions: From **I-81** take exit 205 to Rte. 606 and go west for 1 mile. Winery is on the right. From **northern Virginia** via I-66, take I-81 south. From **Richmond** and **Charlottesville**, take I-64 west to Staunton, then I-81 south. From **Roanoke**, take I-81 north.

Phone: 540-377-6204 or toll-free 888-511-WINE
Fax: 540-377-6204
E-mail: rocwine@cfw.com
Website: www.rockbridgewine.com

Tasting fee: None

Wines: Chardonnay, Riesling, Pinot Noir, Merlot, Chambourcin, late harvest Vidals, *Tuscarora Red*, *Tuscarora White*, *Jeremiah's*, *Vin de Pommes*

Wine related items for sale? Yes
Picnic area? Yes

Owners: Shepherd and Jane Rouse
Winemaker/Viticulturist: Shepherd Rouse

Central Region

44

Barn swallows used to come back every spring to build their nests in the tasting room at Rockbridge Vineyard. That was before the need to air condition forced Jane and Shepherd Rouse to seal off the eaves in the nineteenth-century dairy barn. Jane misses the birds and carefully preserves the remnants of their nests, sturdy little brooding places of mud and thatch built atop a crossbeam or glued, in seemingly miraculous fashion, to a vertical surface. Swallows like barns and similar buildings, and at this winery there is often a chorus of high-pitched singing and twittering going on outside as the birds dart about, scouting for some way to get inside.

In the former milking room shortly after crush, there's a different kind of music to be heard. Barrels of fermenting white wine create a symphony of soft, percolating notes as carbon dioxide bubbles up through clear valves inserted in the bung holes. During fermentation, Jane explains, the yeast turns the sugars in the juice to alcohol and the by-product is CO_2, which needs to be vented. At the same time the winemaker doesn't want any oxygen to get into the barrels. The "bubblers" are partially filled with water, and as carbon dioxide gas builds, it pushes its way through the liquid and is released. The water immediately falls back down in the coiled tube, preventing any air from entering the barrel. If there are many barrels cooking at one time, Jane says, it can get so noisy in the barrel room that it's hard to carry on a conversation.

After a few weeks, fermentation slows, and the cadence of the bubbling gradually decreases until it finally stops altogether. At this point fermentation is virtually complete. The wine is "still" and so are the bubblers, but as yet you do not have "finished" wine. It is yeasty, cloudy, and still slightly fizzy from residual CO_2. In Germany, in October, they drink this *neuer Wein*, or "new wine," which they also call *Federweisse*. Its effect is not unlike that of champagne, zipping into your bloodstream because of the unexpelled effervescence.

It takes a couple of months for the new wine to completely settle down and settle out. The solid matter in the wine and the dead yeast cells fall to the bottom of the barrel. The clear wine can then be siphoned, or "racked," off and the lees cleaned out and discarded. "A lot of what we do throughout the year," says Jane, "is moving the wine from one vessel to another."

Shepherd Rouse has a master's degree in enology from U.C. Davis in California, but his interest in wine was first piqued when, as a boy living in Williamsburg, he discovered what turned out to be the second-oldest dated wine bottle ever found in Virginia. He donated the green bottle, embossed with the year 1718, to the Colonial Williamsburg Foundation. Years later, while touring wine cellars in Germany, the geology major from Washington and Lee University decided he'd rather become a winemaker.

The bar in Shepherd's dairy-barn tasting room is made of rough-sawn wooden planks laid on top of upright barrels. The wines you'll taste here include the very dry, the very sweet, and everything in between. Several styles of Chardonnay and Riesling appear on the list, along with red varietals Pinot Noir, Cabernet Sauvignon, Merlot, and Chambourcin. Specialty wines include Shep's *Vin de Pommes*, a semi-dry, barrel-fermented apple wine, and two late harvest Vidals—the usual sweet interpretation, and a supersweet variation on the theme.

One of the most interesting wines to sample at Rockbridge is a rosé made from French hybrids and the dark blue, native American Concord. Like most boys, the youthful

Shep was fascinated with frogs. When he grew up, he named this Concord blend after the most famous bullfrog of all. The unmistakable aromas and flavors in *Jeremiah's* bring back memories of the best way to eat a Concord grape: Pinch the skin and pop the pale green pulp into your mouth. At the same time that intense flavor and sweetness create an acute taste event on your tongue, the grape's excruciating sourness sinks its talons into the back of your jaws just behind your ears. The denouement to this extreme experience is to chew on the skin, extracting residual sensations of sweet and tart—and the cleansing astringency of tannins that ready your palate for the next explosively delicious grape.

In the finest tradition of amphibian generosity, Rockbridge offers an ample selection of wines to pair with life's many pleasures—wine to enjoy with food, wine to enjoy with friends, and wine to enjoy with your cat curled up in your lap. As the expansive frog would say, *Joie de vivre* to you and me.

Rose River Vineyards

Rose River Vineyards and Trout Farm
Route 648, Box 186
Syria, VA 22743

Hours: 11 a.m. to 5 p.m. Saturday and Sunday from April through November. Other times by appointment. Trout farm and catch-out ponds open Saturday and Sunday from March through October.

Directions: From **Richmond** (via I-64) and **Charlottesville**, take Rte. 29 north to Madison. Turn north (left) onto Rte. 231, then left onto Rte. 670. At Syria, continue west on Rte. 670, passing Graves Mountain Lodge. Turn left onto Rte. 648 to winery entrance. From **D.C.**, take I-66 west to Rte. 29 south. At Madison, take Rte. 231 north (right) to Rte. 670 west to Syria and follow the directions above.

Phone: 540-923-4050

Tasting fee: None

Wines: Cabernet Sauvignon, Chardonnay, Riesling, Mead, *Mountain Peach, Mountain Pear,* and Hungarian Green

Wine related items for sale? Yes
Picnic area? Yes
Food available? Light snacks

Owners: Ken McCoy, Sr. and Ken McCoy, Jr.
Winemaker: Ken McCoy, Jr.

You'll discover this perfectly charming winery where Struthers Run curves north to meet the Rose River at a horseshoe bend near the little town of Syria. The vineyards were founded by Dr. Kenneth McCoy and his son, Ken, Jr.

In 1976 the McCoys planted three acres of vines on their 177-acre tract of hilly terrain at 1,000 feet above sea level. They started with 2,000 vines—200 each of ten varieties. There are now fourteen acres—the original three at the winery site and another eleven on two nearby properties they own. They grow both viniferas and hybrids, including Chardonnay, Riesling, Merlot, Cabernet Sauvignon, Seyval, and Vidal. There's also a very interesting grape you've probably not encountered before called Hungarian Green.

Dr. McCoy is the retired chief of pathology at a Washington, D.C. hospital. Ken, Jr., the winemaker at Rose River, has been in agriculture for many years. At one time he was a crop duster. Later he owned a vine propagation and grafting business in partnership with Joachim Hollerith, former winemaker at Prince Michel. Today Ken concentrates on the vineyards and winery, and on the trout farm and catch-out pond next door.

This is a small winery doing things in a small, often unconventional way. Their press is not the usual bladder type found at most wineries but a vertical hydraulic press that uses a downward motion to squeeze the juice of the grapes through a sieve into a drip pan below. It stays outside on the lattice-enclosed crush pad, a concrete addition to the old stone-foundation barn which houses the winery. Bottling, corking, and labeling are all done by hand. Rose River has never used paper labels. Instead, all of their bottles are silk-screened. This has proved to be a successful marketing tool for the winery, which does private-labeling for weddings, birthdays, and similar functions, as well as for commercial customers.

The tasting *house* at Rose River, just a few yards from the winery, is the original farm dwelling—a tiny structure with just two rooms, one up and one down. When the McCoys renovated it, they had to replace the badly weathered siding, but the frame and the roof are original. So are the stone chimney and the foundation, which were chinked with mud when the house was built in the late 1770s but which the McCoys have since filled with mortar.

The stone fireplace inside also had to be mortared. On a very busy Sunday afternoon, the raised hearth at the opposite end of the room makes a good place to sit and wait your turn at the bar. Or you can use the time to leaf through the winery album, which contains a complete photographic record of the original building and the restoration process. A lighted cabinet on a side wall displays examples of bottles the winery has silkscreened for some of its private-label customers, including the USS *Briscoe*.

The base of the bar is a glass showcase containing arrowheads and other artifacts found on the property. You can study these specimens of early native American craftsmanship while you taste Ken's finely crafted wines. Varietals and blends from the vinifera and hybrid grapes listed above are offered, as well as several fruit wines—including peach and apple—and a honey mead. Dr. McCoy thinks the Hungarian Green bears a strong resemblance to Chardonnay, with the latter coming across as a bit timid by comparison. When available—it isn't every year—the peppery varietal in the green bottle provides a unique and enjoyable new taste experience and might aptly be described as Chardonnay with an attitude.

The McCoys have laid a patio next to the tasting house. This is a wonderful place for adjusting your own attitude, if it needs it, while you sip Ken's wines and listen to the bullfrogs. The lily pads in the pond at the bottom of the hill are favorite jumping off places, and the big frogs are especially vocal in the spring. If you're not familiar with the sound, you may at first think it's a horn of sorts, or some kind of light artillery.

The winery is open on Saturdays and Sundays, during which there seems to be a steady stream of customers in and out of the tasting house. When asked how the USS *Briscoe* knew about the little winery tucked way up in the hills, Dr. McCoy was heard to reply, "Everybody knows about us. You're the last one to find out." That's probably not quite true. Chances are *you're* the last to find out, in which case you'll want to visit Rose River as soon as possible and experience the delightful scenery, sounds, and wines you've been missing.

Sharp Rock Vineyards

Sharp Rock Vineyards
5 Sharp Rock Road
Sperryville, VA 22740

Hours: 1 p.m. to 5 p.m. on Fridays and Sundays and noon to 5 p.m. on Saturdays from March through December. Open Memorial Day, Labor Day, and Columbus Day from 1 p.m. to 5 p.m.

Directions: From **D.C.** area, take I-66 west to Gainesville, then Rte. 29 south to Warrenton. Exit at Business 29 to Warrenton. Follow signs to Rte. 211. Take Rte. 211 west for 28 miles to Sperryville, then turn left on Rte. 522 into town and follow signs to Rte. 231 (about 1/2 mile). Turn right on Rte. 231 and go 8 miles to Rte. 601. Turn right and go just over 1 mile to intersection of Rtes. 601 and 707. Sharp Rock Farm is on the right, across the Hughes River Bridge. From **Charlottesville,** take Rte. 29 north to Madison. Turn left (north) onto Rte. 231 and go about 12 miles to Rte. 601. Turn left and follow directions above.

Phone: 540-987-9700
Fax: 540-987-9031
E-mail: darmor@sharprock-vineyards.com
Website: www.sharprockvineyards.com

Tasting fee: $2 per person, applied to wine purchase

Wines: Chardonnay, Sauvignon Blanc, Cabernet Sauvignon, Cabernet Franc, Malbec

Wine related items for sale? Yes
Picnic area? Yes
Food available? Light snacks

Owners: David and Marilyn Armor
Winemaker: David Armor

Old Rag Mountain creates an imposing, rough-hewn backdrop for David Armor's winery near Sperryville, in Rappahannock County. In spring, the narrow Hughes River coursing through the property sends torrents of water over the rocky river bed. It is the source for the drip irrigation system used when conditions in the vineyards become extreme, and according to David, the river never runs dry, even in times of severe drought.

In the early nineties David had only a passing awareness of Virginia's reemerging wine industry. While eating out, he discovered that the local restaurant where he was dining had its own on-site vineyard and was sending the grapes to a nearby winery to be vinted and private-labeled. It occurred to David that his place in the country might be suitable for growing grapes as well. The assessment made by the state viticulturist, Dr. Tony Wolf, was favorable, and his advice was to start with a five-acre trial plot. David planted three acres, and when these did well, he planted another two.

At present David grows only vinifera varieties from which he produces only dry wines. He usually has two Chardonnays, both barrel fermented in French oak. One is a crisper, fruitier style of wine that he does not put through malolactic conversion. Fifty percent of the wine in the reserve Chardonnay, however, has been through ML and expresses the characteristic buttery finish that results when malic acid is changed to the softer lactic acid during this secondary fermentation process. David also produces three Bordeaux reds—Cabernet Sauvignon, Malbec, and Cabernet Franc. These wines are not permitted to "cold soak"—to sit on the skins after fermentation is complete in order to extract more color and tannins. Rather, as soon as the wine is dry—when all the sugar has been converted to alcohol—it is immediately pressed off. As a result, while there is a modest astringency on the finish, the tannins in David's red wines are generally soft and subdued.

David and Marilyn Armor believe they have found a little bit of heaven in their twenty-three acres at the foot of the Blue Ridge Mountains. Sharp Rock Farm was established in 1794, and the Armors' parcel contains the original farmhouse, a two-story starter "cottage" built in 1795. The main house, a three-story frame structure completed in the 1860s, is occupied by the Armors. The carriage house is perched on an incline to the left of the drive leading to the house and the adjacent cottage. Careful restoration of all three buildings has created a portrait of gracious Southern living that beckons travellers from around the country and the globe. Both the cottage and the carriage house are part of a year-round bed and breakfast operation at Sharp Rock Farm.

There's a cherry tree growing next to the carriage house that must be very old indeed; its branches hang so low they nearly sweep the grassy bank that falls off sharply towards the stream below. In late June the huge tree is weighted down with fruit. Guests can stand on the deck and lose themselves in a pastoral reverie induced by delectably sweet and sour cherries plucked right off the tree and the musical renditions of the Hughes River at the bottom of the slope.

Renovation of the barn which houses the winery posed a unique challenge for the Armors. Blown over in a windstorm, it had to be completely taken apart and put back together.

Some of the poplar siding had to be replaced, but the majority of the original boards, posts, and beams were saved. The production area is on the ground floor. A post in one corner bears an inscription that leaves no question as to the age of the structure. Inscribed with the date 1890, it also identifies the builder as Weldon Americus Yowell. His ancestor Johannas Yowell was a Confederate soldier in the Fourth Virginia Cavalry and is buried in the cemetery at the top of a hill overlooking the vineyards. You can view both the vineyards and the cemetery through the wide windows of the enclosed deck just off the tasting room.

Ten-inch heart pine floor boards from a log cabin in North Carolina provide visitors with secure footing in the tasting room, which is upstairs in the former hayloft. The bar top is made of planks from a black walnut tree that was growing just outside the barn corral. Before becoming the elegant counter where his wines are sampled, the solid walnut boards were aged for just over a year—not quite as long as David's Chardonnays.

Sharp Rock Vineyards is one of Virginia's newest wineries, having opened its doors in September of 1998. It offers a taste of carefully handcrafted wines from a dedicated new winemaker and a little sampling of the Armors' earthly paradise, which they happily share with winery visitors and their B & B guests.

Stone Mountain Vineyards

Stone Mountain Vineyards
1376 Wyatt Mountain Road
Dyke, VA 22935

Hours: 11 a.m. to 4 p.m. Saturday and Sunday during March and from November through December; 11 a.m. to 5 p.m. Saturday and Sunday from April through October. Open during January and February, weather permitting. Please call first.

Directions: From **northern Virginia,** take I-66 west to Rte. 29 south to Ruckersville, then Rte. 33 west to Stanardsville. Turn left onto Rte. 810 (Dyke Road) to Dyke, VA. Turn right onto Rte. 627 (Bacon Hollow Road) and go 3.6 miles to Rte. 632 (Wyatt Mountain Road). Turn left and proceed up the mountain for 2 miles to the winery entrance, on the left. From **Charlottesville,** take Rte. 29 north to Ruckersville, then Rte. 33 west to Stanardsville and follow the directions above.

Phone: 804-990-9463
E-mail: info@stonemountain-vineyards.com
Website: www.stonemountain-vineyards.com

Tasting fee: None

Wines: Cabernet Sauvignon, Cabernet Franc, Chardonnay, Riesling, Chasselas Dore, *Bacon Hollow Revenuers' Select*

Picnic area? Yes

Owners: Al and Chris Breiner
Winemaker: Chris Breiner
Consulting Winemaker: Gabriele Rausse

The popular saying "Plan your work and work your plan" could well be the motto for this brand new winery that just opened to the public in June of the year 2000. Stone Mountain Vineyards is owned and operated by the father and son team of Al and Chris Breiner. The winery facility was designed with their ultimate production goal in mind. They knew they wanted to eventually produce 5,000 cases a year, so they visited other wineries to determine the right size—in terms of square footage—and built their winery to accommodate projected volume, thus precluding the need for costly alterations in the future.

Al's background as a patent attorney may have something to do with the emphasis at Stone Mountain on detailed planning, sound design, and most importantly, having a good product. The Breiners ensured they would have an outstanding selection of wines from the very start by engaging Gabriele Rausse as consulting winemaker. Rausse has been showing Virginians how to make wine since arriving here from his native Italy in 1976. He was the first winemaker at Barboursville, where he established one of the earliest vinifera vineyards in the state in modern times. Later, at what is now Jefferson Vineyards, he planted vinifera vines and made wine on land where his ancestral countryman Filippo Mazzei had attempted to grow European grapes for Thomas Jefferson. Today, Gabriele is assistant director in charge of grounds and gardens at Monticello, Jefferson's magnificent neoclassical home overlooking Jefferson Vineyards and the city of Charlottesville. He continues to assist other Virginia wineries, while vinting and marketing his own wines as well.

With Rausse's help, Chris Breiner has submitted an inaugural list of wines that will have delighted patrons not thinking twice about making the trip up Wyatt Mountain time and time again. Current vinifera varietals include a gentle giant—a hefty, but softly tannic Cabernet Sauvignon reserve without what Chris terms that "dusty" taste often exhibited by a Cabernet. Aging it half in American and half in French barrels gives the *Chardonnay Reserve* unmistakable, but not overpowering, oakiness. It's also fruity and crisp and lightly spread with butter. Stone Mountain offers two Rieslings: One is a semi-sweet with about 4 percent residual sugar that seems less sweet than it is because it's so nicely balanced on the acid side. The other is an ultra-dry Riesling with residual sugar in, as Chris puts it, the negative digits. "Rieslings in particular are known for picking up the different minerals in the vineyard," he says. The uniqueness of the terroir in which the grapes for this wine were planted is exhibited in an astringency, an almost tannic quality that adds interest without masking the fruit and floral notes so abundant in a Riesling.

Chasselas Dore is a Swiss grape, one of the many European varieties Thomas Jefferson attempted to grow at Monticello. Stone Mountain is producing a varietal from the Chasselas Dore, maximizing the natural fruitiness of the wine by fermenting and aging it entirely in stainless steel.

Bacon Hollow, where the Breiner's have their place, is just west of Mutton Hollow on Virginia State Route 810. While the Breiners are not the first to make alcoholic beverages in Bacon Hollow, they are, according to Chris and the ABC Board, the first to do so legally. Years ago, the hollow was known for producing some of the best white lightning to be had in Virginia. It's no wonder government agents spent what to the inhabitants must have seemed like an inordinate amount of time here. The Chasselas Dore grape is the basis of a nearly celestial semi-dry white wine that the Breiners call *Bacon Hollow Revenuers' Select* and have dedicated "to moonshiners and the revenuers who pursued them."

The massive deck that wraps around two sides of the tasting room is the perfect place to enjoy a glass of *Revenuers' Select* while toasting both the seekers and the sought-after in Greene County's not so distant beverage-making past. On a slope just below the winery is a small vineyard, three acres out of the fifteen acres of grapes currently planted in four different spots on this 650-acre mountain farm. On an early summer's evening, with the sun arcing down on the other side, it's cool in the shadow of the tasting room looking east into the broad, still well-lit valley, while closer by row after row of neatly hedged vines turns deeper shades of green in the declining light.

To the right of the vineyard, a rugged dirt road winds downward into Bacon Hollow, skirting past a pair of stony relics: chimney ruins facing off like duelers that have come here to settle some old matter in a wooded setting.

Inside the tasting room, a phalanx of ceiling fans keep a nice breeze going, fending off the need to switch on the air conditioning. The interior is entirely paneled in wood—floors, walls, and ceilings. The bar is in the center of the main room, with wide-open areas of ballroom proportions on either side. Underneath all this, a huge crush pad—the Breiners call it the apron—is protected from downpours by the overhanging deck. The ample-sized production area opens onto the pad on one side, and on the other it leads into the barrel cave under the mountain.

The plan for this winery has been carefully unfolding since the seventies when Al saw grapes being grown along Germany's Rhine River and reasoned he could do the same on his farm in Virginia. Reflecting on the wines, the view, the facilities, and the wonderful hospitality visitors will experience here, it can be said without hesitation that the Breiners' plan works.

Stonewall Vineyards & Winery

Stonewall Vineyards
and Winery
RR 2, Box 107A
Concord, VA 24538

Hours: 11 a.m. to 5 p.m. daily, except New Year's Day, Easter, July 4th, Thanksgiving, and Christmas Day.

Directions: From **Lynchburg**, go 12 miles east on Rte. 460. At Concord light, go north 5 miles on Rte. 608. Turn left onto Rte. 721 and go 100 yards to winery entrance, on the left.

Phone: 804-993-2185
Fax: 804-993-3975
E-mail: stonewallwine@juno.com

Tasting fee: None

Wines: Chardonnay, Merlot, Cabernet Sauvignon, Chambourcin, Vidal Blanc, claret, *Cayuga White, Brigade, Pyment* (mead)

Wine related items for sale? Yes
Picnic area? Yes
Food available? Light snacks
Special Programs? Winemaker Dinners
Facilities for private functions? Yes

Owners: Larry and Sterry Davis
Winemaker/Viticulturist: Bart Davis

Bring your camera when you visit this winery, and make sure you have plenty of color film. The grounds at Stonewall Vineyards were planted with year-round color in mind. The pear trees blossom first, sometimes as early as mid March. Redbud, azaleas, dogwood, and crepe myrtle all have their turn as the season carefully unfolds its multihued tapestry in the semi-enclosed courtyard. A hybrid variety of day lily blooms practically all year long. In autumn, October Glory maples preparing for winter's hibernation casually drop their robes of vibrant red and yellow onto the deep-piled, bright green carpet beneath their boughs.

Sixteen acres of vines surround the main building, whose strung-out architecture and pale facade can put you somewhat in mind of a hacienda. A cool arcade leads from the tasting room to the winery and is studded along the way with vintage winemaking equipment, and a reproduction Civil War cannon.

Inside the winery, the humidity in the barrel room matches that of a muggy Virginia summer day, but the cool fifty-five-degree temperature keeps the moist air from becoming oppressive. A constant 92 percent relative humidity is just what the barrels need to keep them from losing wine through evaporation. Over a year or two, this can save as much as a case of wine per barrel, according to winemaker Bart Davis—not an insignificant amount when you consider the retail price of twelve bottles of a premium Chardonnay or Cabernet varietal.

Bart is also the viticulturist at this midsized winery, which means that much of his time is spent on vineyard management. The season and the weather determine the schedule. In the spring it can be seven days a week—from 5:30 A.M. until about 1:00, to take advantage of the cooler morning hours. "Some days," says Bart, "we can work fourteen hours." Other days it can be considerably less.

Bart, whose parents, Larry and Sterry Davis, own Stonewall Vineyards, has been making wine for a little over a decade. During that time he has seen a discernable difference in the growing season in this part of the state, especially in recent years when it's been much drier than normal. "This has produced grapes that are fruitier and more aromatic," he says, "yielding wines with a better nose and a better mouth feel due to more concentration of grape than water. Vines that are under stress for water produce better fruit."

In addition to the sixteen acres surrounding the winery, Stonewall leases an additional thirty acres of vines. Production at the winery has risen from 900 annual cases when the Davises bought it in 1990 to 6,000, with 10,000 cases being the ultimate goal. Traffic at the winery has nearly tripled since the new tasting room was built in 1997. A trio of delicately wrought chandeliers suspended from the wood-beamed cathedral ceiling guides your eyes down the center of the quarry-tiled room to the fireplace at the opposite end. A diverted glance to the right discovers the new barrel cave and wine library. This small room with its vaulted ceiling and arched iron gate has a decidedly monastic aura about it. You half expect to see a cassocked friar appear, take a seat at the table, and begin scribing something on a piece of parchment.

Perhaps it would be instructions for making Pyment, a honey-mead wine they make at Stonewall using an authentic fourteenth-century English recipe. It calls for blending grape wine and mead with peppercorns, cloves, and oil of bergamot. Sunk deep in the leather sofa in front of the towering granite fireplace, sipping a glass of this favorite medieval quaff, you'll soon be toasting the mead maker as roundly as a Saxon nobleman.

If you're from New York, you'll appreciate that Stonewall makes a wine from your state's favorite grape, the hybrid Cayuga, and that this semi-dry varietal is their best selling wine.

Stonewall Vineyards is located in Appomattox County not far from where Robert E. Lee surrendered to Ulysses S. Grant, bringing the Civil War to an end. Regardless of where we're from, here, within a few miles of where he laid down his sword, we can raise a glass to the beloved General Lee—and at the same time thank our lucky stars that Virginia is still part of the great nation whose character and destiny she has played such a vital role in shaping.

The tiny village of Stonewall is in a very rural area, and the town itself keeps getting smaller. Where there was once a general store, a hardware store, a school, and a church, only the church remains. The Davises used to worry that, from a business perspective, they were too far off the beaten path. Now they find that people enjoy the drive through the countryside to get to their winery. Their farm and Bart's farm join to create 500 acres of gently rolling peace and quiet. "We're in our own little world down here," says Bart. And what a nice little world it is.

White Hall Vineyards

White Hall Vineyards 5184 Sugar Ridge Road White Hall, VA 22987 **Hours:** 11 a.m. to 5 p.m. Wednesday through Sunday. Closed on Easter, Thanksgiving, and from December 15 through February. **Directions:** From **Route 29 in Charlottesville,** go west on Barracks Road (which becomes Garth Road) to White Hall. Take Rte. 810 north, then left onto Breakheart (Rte. 674) and continue to Sugar Ridge Road. Go 1/2 mile to winery, on the right. From **I-64,** take Crozet exit, then Rte. 250 east. Turn left onto Rte. 240, then take Rte. 810 to White Hall. Continue north on 810 and follow directions above. **Phone:** 804-823-8615 **E-mail:** tastingroom@whitehallvineyards.com **Website:** www.whitehallvineyards.com **Tasting fee:** None **Wines:** Cabernet Sauvignon, Cabernet Franc, Merlot, Chardonnay, Gewürztraminer, *Soliterre, Cuvée de Champs, Sugar Ridge White* **Wine related items for sale?** Yes **Picnic area?** Yes **Facilities for private functions?** Yes **Owners:** Antony and Edith Champ **Winemaker:** Bradford McCarthy **Farm Manager:** D. Scott Cruden	If horticulture is your passion, or if you just like a pretty yard, you'll love what Edie and Antony Champ have done at their winery. Soon after it opened in 1994, they hired a landscape architect to decorate the grounds using only trees, shrubs, and plants that are native to the eastern United States. In the ensuing years the landscaping has matured nicely, and so has the winery. The original basement facility, now the barrel room, has developed into an impressive three-storied structure. California and Virginia architects both worked on the design. Tony declines to put a label on the architectural style, but the stucco facade definitely imparts a West Coast flavor. The red metal roof, on the other hand, reminds you of those wonderful old tin roofs that once provided such excellent cover for most of Virginia's farm dwellings and outbuildings. The tasting room, on the ground floor, borders on the enormous. There's a fireplace near the entrance, and hanging just above it is a landscape schematic of the original plantings where horticulture buffs can verify the identifications they make on their way up the sidewalk. The octagonal bar is in the center of the room, across a cool, quarry-stone floor. Fountains accent each corner at the other end of the room, where french doors open onto an interior balcony that overlooks the tank room. The Champs refer to the space on the winery's upper level as the party room. You can get a good echo in this long, tall, sparsely but elegantly furnished chamber. Wooden beams in the cathedral ceiling, chandeliers, and solid oak planks covered with oriental rugs—and another stone fireplace—tempt you to dub this full-story event room the Great Hall. While it will charm you with its pleasing architecture and graceful landscaping, White Hall Vineyards is much more than just a pretty face. An inside balcony on the second story offers the same view as the one in the tasting room, but from a higher elevation. If you stand here long enough, you're almost certain to catch a glimpse of Brad McCarthy. This talented young winemaker, who grew up in Charlottesville, has earned White Hall the nearly unprecedented distinction of winning Virginia's coveted Governor's Cup two years in a

row. What's truly remarkable is that the winery was only two vintages old when it took its first Cup—in 1996 for its 1995 Cabernet Sauvignon. The following year their Gewürztraminer topped the list at the annual competition.

The standard tour at White Hall starts outside on the crush pad. If you're here during harvest, you may well get to see the wine press in action. A rubber bladder inside inflates, squeezing whole clusters of Chardonnay grapes against the sides until the fragrant juice comes streaming out through thousands of tiny holes in the walls of the press, pouring into the catch pan as freely as the winemaker's promises of something better yet to come. For those who visit at other times of the year, White Hall has an engaging audio-visual presentation. The audio: your guide's exceptionally lucid explanation of the steps involved in wine grape processing. The supporting video: a hefty album loaded with vivid color photos taken at the winery during crush.

If you're wondering why a winemaker would press an entire bunch of grapes—without destemming and crushing them first—they'll tell you at White Hall that as soon as a grape is crushed, the juice from the pulp begins to extract components, such as tannins, from the skins. When making red wines this is desirable, but for white wines it often is not. With whole-cluster, or whole-berry, pressing, the juice spends minimal time in contact with the skins. Likewise, the cold juice from white grapes that have been chilled overnight in a refrigerated truck extracts less from the skins than the warm juice of grapes right off the vine.

From the crush pad you'll enter White Hall's tank room. The dimpled areas on the tall stainless steel containers are refrigeration jackets where a cold glycol solution is circulated to control the rate of fermentation. Heat is a natural by-product of fermentation, which if allowed to proceed unchecked can lead to a boiling off of some of the wine's nicer aromas and flavors. It's much like the difference between cooking a pot of soup at a slow simmer and rushing it to doneness at a fast boil.

The barrel room is dim and cool and atmospheric with its low, beamed ceiling and thick, rough-hewn supporting timbers. There's a smattering of seldom-encountered thin-staved barrels, which allow more air to penetrate the oak, resulting in subtle flavor changes that they like here at White Hall. You'll recognize them by the reinforcing planks on the barrel heads. Periodically, at night, the entire room is cloaked in a man-made fog that keeps the barrels from drying out and losing too much wine through evaporation.

White Hall currently grows Chardonnay, Cabernet Sauvignon and Cabernet Franc, Merlot, Gewürztraminer, and Pinot Gris. There's a small lot of Muscat and Touriga, and an exquisite new block of Petit Verdot visible from the south-facing balcony on the winery's second floor. They buy all their Vidal, which they use to make a simulated late harvest delight they call *Soliterre.* Instead of allowing the grapes to continue to hang to increase the Brix level, or sugar content, they pick them as soon as they are technically ripe and freeze them. The grapes are then partially thawed and pressed. The juice yield is about 60 percent of what you would normally get, but since much of the water remains behind as ice crystals, the must is highly concentrated with sugars and flavors.

Starting in the mid-sixties Edie and Tony Champ tried several times to grow their own wine grapes, planting ten or twenty vines at a time. But as soon as the vines were mature enough to bear, Tony—whose last nonfarm job was as president and CEO of a synthetic fibers company—would get transferred. They now have 25 acres of vineyards on a 300-acre parcel, with plans to double their plantings to 50 acres, a fitting conclusion to their decades-long pursuit of a dream—and reasonable compensation for the grapes they had to leave behind.

White Hall Vineyards

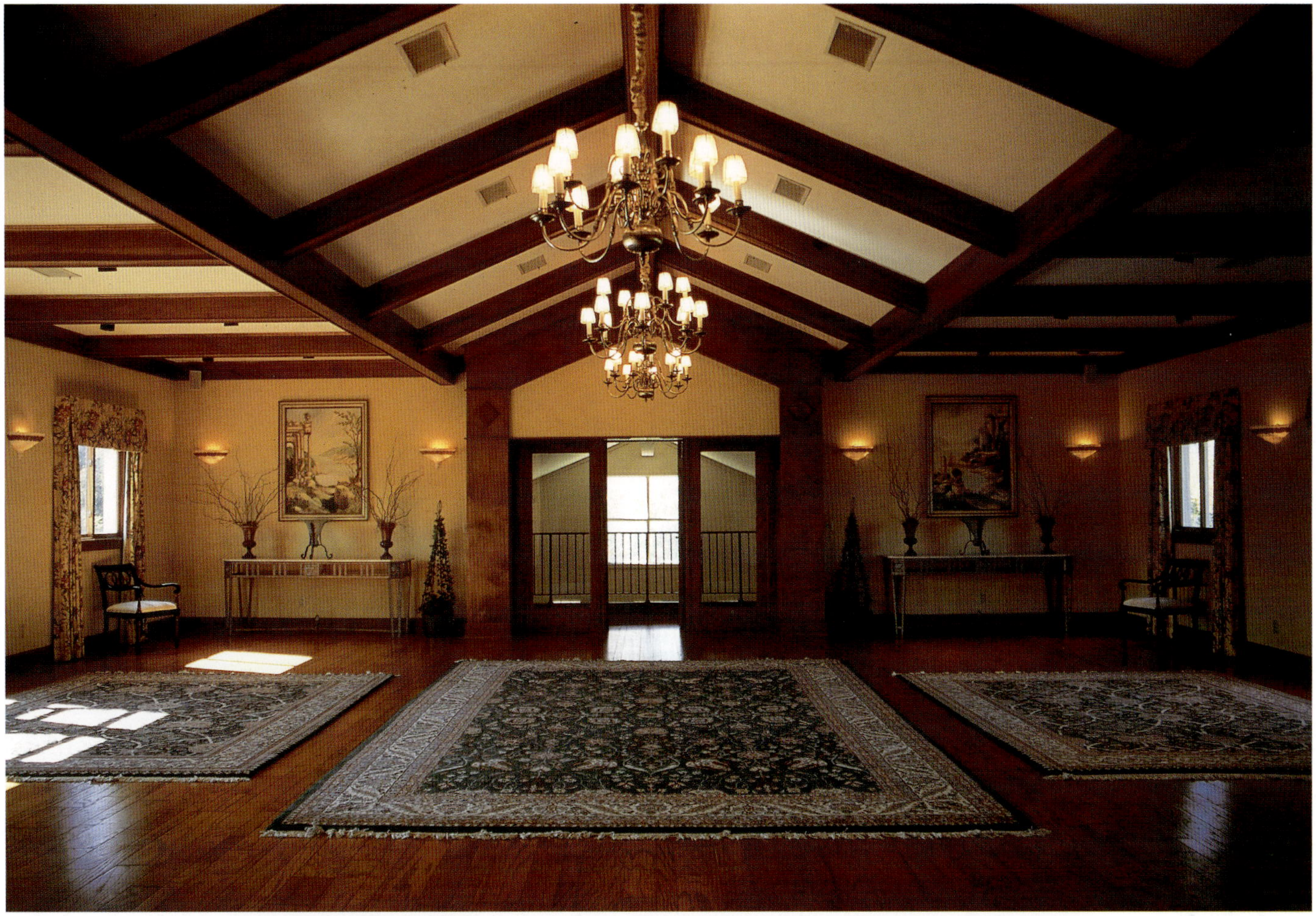

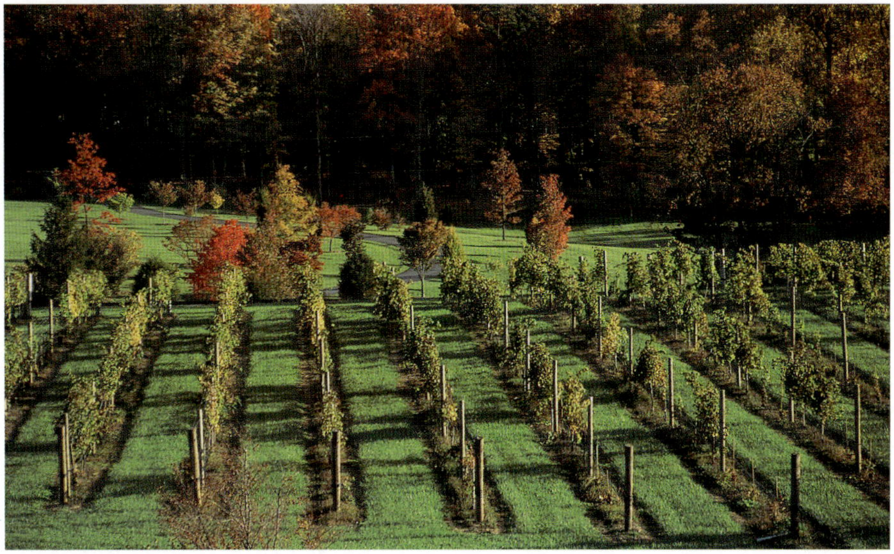

Wintergreen Winery

Wintergreen Winery
462 Winery Lane
Nellysford, VA 22958

Hours: 10 a.m. to 6 p.m. daily from April through October. 10 a.m. to 5 p.m. daily from November through March. Closed Thanksgiving, Christmas Day, and New Year's Day.

Directions: From **Blue Ridge Parkway,** exit at Reed's Gap onto Rte. 664 east and go 5 miles. Winery is on the left. From **Richmond** and **Charlottesville,** take I-64 west to exit 107, then Rte. 250 west to Rte. 151. Go south on Rte. 151 for 14 miles and take Rte. 664 west for 1/2 mile to winery entrance, on the right.

Phone: 804-361-2519
Fax: 804-361-1510
Website: www.wintergreenwinery.com

Tasting fee: None

Wines: Cabernet Sauvignon, Chardonnay, Riesling, Merlot, Raspberry dessert wine, *Thomas Nelson White, Three Ridges Red, Mill Hill Apple Wine*

Wine related items for sale? Yes
Picnic area? Yes
Food available? Light snacks

Owners: Jeff and Tamara Stone
Winemaker/Viticulturist: Jeff Stone

The Rockfish River in June is an unassuming little brook where it trickles through the portion of Mill Hill Farm where the Wintergreen vineyards are planted. The smooth-worn boulders that fill the river bed, however, are a testimony to nature's sometimes violent episodes—like Hurricane Camille's rampage across the south Virginia highlands in August of 1969. The presence in the stream of this "river jack" provides a narrow, cautionary revelation of the true makeup of the surrounding terrain—a rock-littered substrate barely concealed by a thin layer of topsoil. It's tough going for many crops, but grapes pay it little mind. In 1989 Wintergreen's founders, Mike and Kathy Riddick, planted vinifera vines in this rugged terroir. Three years later they had their first vintage, and the following year they opened their winery.

In April of 1999 Jeff Stone and his wife, Tammy, purchased the vineyards and the winery. Jeff grew up in the Finger Lakes region of New York, where that state's winemaking industry is concentrated. After several years as a national accounts manager for a large, international frozen foods manufacturer, he traded in his round trips on big planes for round trips up and down rows of vines on a small tractor. "You have to be very serious about the wine business if you're going to farm grapes," says Jeff. "It takes a lot of work." These days, he believes, Virginia is attracting people to the business who fully understand what is involved. That's really why the quality of Virginia wines has reached its current state of excellence and why he thinks it will continue to improve.

Some of the work Jeff speaks of is just making sure his efforts in the fields are not undone by any number of natural challenges faced by most Virginia winegrowers. A regular schedule of spraying is essential to protect the vines from plant disease and pests and thus ensure the development of a healthy and bountiful crop. Jeff uses owl decoys in his vineyards and has also set a number of hawk perches among his vines to attract the natural enemy of other birds that would prey upon the defenseless fruit.

Groundhogs can be extremely destructive, digging up holes in the vineyards and damaging roots. Foxes move in and evict the groundhogs, who have to dig new holes. Having been offered these insights, we can begin to fully appreciate what grape farmers must go through to give us good wine. Between the $650 French oak barrels and all that "varmint" hunting—as Jeff puts it—it hardly behooves any of us to complain about the price of a bottle of premium Chardonnay.

Mill Hill Farm dates back to the mid-1700s and was part of a vast plantation in the Rockfish Valley owned by the Rodes family. This particular farm developed into the apple-growing division of their far-flung agribusiness. The winery is in a more than 200-year-old apple-packing shed, and the hands-on winemaking here has been adapted so as not to disturb the original layout of the building.

On Jeff's tour you'll get a detailed explanation of how fermentation works and learn that while mankind has been making wine for over 8,000 years, it was only in the last two centuries that we discovered how the alcohol got into the juice. This winemaker knows when he's getting a vigorous secondary fermentation—or malolactic conversion—in his Chardonnay because the plastic bungs start popping out of their holes as carbon dioxide pressure builds inside the barrels. Special one-way air locks, called bubblers, are then inserted into the holes to let the CO_2 out and keep oxygen from getting in. During fermentation constant monitoring of temperature is necessary. With raspberry wine, for example, fermentation can become much too robust, building so much heat that it kills the yeast and self-destructs. To avoid having to reinoculate, the tanks have to be periodically chilled down.

Many people who come to the winery are in the area to enjoy the outdoor activities that attract visitors to Nelson County during all four seasons of the year. The ski resort at Wintergreen is just four miles away on the same state route as the vineyards. After a tour and a tasting, you can select from a list that includes estate-bottled vinifera and hybrid varietals and blends, as well as fruit wines like their raspberry—which is highly recommended with chocolate—and apple wine made from Winesap and Golden Delicious apples.

The well-stocked gift shop here contains every wine-related thing you need to facilitate a pleasant interlude with a fine Virginia wine from Wintergreen Winery, whether it's *après* ski at the resort or *après* a day at work when the outing is over.

Ingleside Plantation Vineyards

Ingleside Plantation Vineyards
5872 Leedstown Road
Oak Grove, VA 22443

Hours: 10 a.m. to 5 p.m. Monday through Saturday. Noon to 5 p.m. on Sunday. Closed Thanksgiving, Christmas, and New Year's Day.

Directions: Located midway between Washington, D.C. and Richmond off Rte. 301. From **Rte. 301,** go east on Rte. 3 for 10 miles and turn right onto Rte. 638 (Leedstown Road). Go 2.5 miles to winery, on the left.

Phone: 804-224-8687
Fax: 804-224-8573
E-mail: mail@ipwine.com
Website: www.ipwine.com

Tasting fee: None

Wines: Cabernet Sauvignon, Cabernet Franc, Sangiovese, Merlot, Chardonnay, Viognier, brut sparkling wine

Wine related items for sale? Yes
Picnic area? Yes
Food available? Light snacks; light luncheon fare when tour buses are running
Special Programs? George Washington Wine Society
Facilities for private functions? Yes

Owner: Doug Flemer
Winemaker: Stephen Rigby
Viticulturist: Matt Chobanian

The Northern Neck is a 100-mile-long peninsula between the Potomac on the northeast and the Rappahannock on the southwest, with both rivers emptying into the Chesapeake Bay. All of its five million acres once belonged to Lord Fairfax, northern Virginia's preeminent eighteenth-century landlord. George Washington was born here, and so was Robert E. Lee. It was one of the first areas explored by Captain John Smith, and Pocahontas was supposedly captured here by the English and taken to Jamestown.

Ingleside Plantation Vineyards is located at the narrowest part of the peninsula and also on its highest ground. Its elevation of 190 feet above sea level falls considerably short of the recommended 800 to 1,200 feet. The land is surprisingly hilly, though, and the wind currents created by two of the state's major rivers, as well as the sandy, loamy soil reminiscent of Bordeaux, actually equate to very favorable grape growing conditions here in the Tidewater region of Virginia.

Carl Flemer, whose great grandfather bought the former plantation in 1890, began to shift away from traditional dairy farming in the 1940s when he started a nursery on the 3,000-acre tract. Ingleside is now home to one of the largest suppliers of ornamental shrubbery on the East Coast. In the late seventies, having successfully grown a few grapes and made a little wine for family and friends, Carl decided to explore the possibilities of producing Virginia wines commercially.

In 1980 Jacques Recht, a renowned European enologist, and his wife Liliane were sailing around the world in their homemade catamaran. Jacques had been reading James Michener's *Chesapeake* and wanted to see the famous inlet

for himself. In a small bayshore town fate brought the retired wine expert and the venture winemaker together. Jacques agreed to help Carl at his new winery "for a little while." This temporary commitment turned into a long-term association spanning more than a decade. During that time Ingleside won the Virginia Governor's Cup two years back to back, making it one of only two wineries to achieve that distinction. Jacques, who originally planned to settle in the south of England, now lives permanently in the southern U.S. Since leaving Ingleside, he has acted as consulting pioneer to many of Virginia's new wineries, helping them, as one Ingleside staff member put it, "figure out what to do with where they were."

Doug Flemer, Carl's son, is president of the winery operation and studied winemaking in both California and France. In recent years he has cut the annual cases produced at Ingleside from 20,000 to around 12,000 in order to concentrate on creating the highest quality wines possible from their current seventy acres of vinifera and French hybrid varieties. Vineyardist Matt Chobanian and winemaker Stephen Rigby have together fashioned a list of over twenty different wines consistent with Ingleside's mission of getting more Americans to try, appreciate, and become regular patrons of domestically vinted wines. Their potential converts are many. Notes Ingleside's retail manager, Garry Keckley, "Ninety percent of the wine produced in this country is consumed by only 10 percent of its people."

The Ingleside list is divided into four tiers. Their *Chesapeake* series features blended, dry red and white table wines, while the sweeter blends and dessert wines are bottled under the *Colonial* label. The *Premium* series includes the named varietals. Their limited-quantity *Reserves* are varietals that have either spent more time in the barrel or come from a specific block of grapes considered superior to the rest of the vintage.

The winery boasts all the modern winemaking equipment an operation of its size could effectively utilize, yet, Garry admits, at harvest it still employs one very unmodern technique: at Ingleside they still press grapes using the age-old method of stomping. More accurately, their white grapes go into the press whole cluster and a cellar worker in waterman boots climbs inside while it's being filled and walks around a bit to compress the load. Meanwhile, the plasticized canvas bladder in the bottom—which will inflate after the worker climbs out—is cushioned by the layers of grapes on top.

After turning off Route 638, which was once a well-trod Indian trail leading from one side of the peninsula to the other, visitors will travel up a modestly winding drive past several vineyards to the parking area. From here a pair of iron gates swing inward on a European-style courtyard and an entire morning or afternoon of wine-related enjoyment.

The tour starts outside the tasting room in the shadow of two ivy-covered silos attached to what was once the dairy. From here your guide will take you to a newer building which houses the winery and most of Ingleside's stainless steel tanks. You'll learn that, as a rule of thumb, Ingleside's sweeter wines are fermented in stainless and remain in stainless

Ingleside Plantation Vineyards

until bottled. The dry reds are fermented in steel tanks then transferred to American oak barrels for aging. The dry whites, on the other hand, are both fermented and aged in French or American oak of various vintages, depending on how much of an impact the winemaker wants the oak to have. Their *Northern Neck Select Chardonnay,* for example, always goes into brand new American oak, and the impact, while pleasing, is not subtle.

A wide, concrete breezeway connects the winery to the barrel room. During harvest it serves as the crush pad and is crowded with the crusher/destemmer (the first stop for red wine grapes) and the press—plus a constantly shifting array of lugs, pumps, hoses, and grape stompers. At other times the pad pulls duty as the staff's basketball court.

When you cross the pad to the barrel room, you're back at the dairy. There's a two- or three-step climb to a wide platform in the center of the room. Up here big, 110-gallon neutral oak barrels and heavy, solid oak planks serve as a bar for overflow crowds and at special functions like barrel tastings and VIP tours. The lower level perimeter is stacked on one side with conventional fifty-five-gallon barrels filled with aging wine, and there's an engaging shadow box effect created by a quartet of darkly painted arches and soft lighting.

Between the barrel room and the tasting room, there's a charming little space with fireplace and leaded glass window. (In a dairy? you may wonder.) This old-fashioned parlor is furnished with lots of antiques and knickknacks, some of which are for sale. There are many more things to buy in the gift shop, which overflows into the tasting room, which spills out into the courtyard—where there are plenty of tables and chairs, and lots of trees to help you stay cool in even the warmest weather. On chilly days or when it's raining, you can seek the comfort of the fully enclosed, heated pavilion.

One of the most pleasant ways to arrive at Ingleside is via water. Excursion boats leave the town of Tappahannock—on the Rappahannock—for historic Leedstown several days a week. From Leedstown, buses take passengers to the winery for a complimentary tour and tasting, plus a catered lunch. Other visitors can also buy lunch at the winery when the tour groups are here.

You get the impression that the owners of this winery are as committed to preserving the history of the Northern Neck as they are to producing fine wines. The museum directly across the courtyard from the tasting room houses an impressive collection of native American artifacts, everything from arrowheads and axes to ceremonial pipes and knives—all found on or around the plantation site or in the Leedstown environs. A string of Spanish trade beads, the largest and most complete collection discovered in the Western Hemisphere, dates from the late sixteenth or early seventeenth century. While you can't tour the plantation house—it's the private residence of Carl Flemer and his wife Shirley—you can learn about its fascinating and diverse history in the broadcast-quality video the owners have produced about Leedstown and historic Westmoreland County. At Ingleside they're proud of their heritage and proud of their wines—and rightfully so in both cases.

63

Lake Anna Winery

Lake Anna Winery
5621 Courthouse Road
Spotsylvania, VA 22553

Hours: 11 a.m. to 5 p.m. Wednesday through Saturday, and 1 p.m. to 5 p.m. on Sunday from April through December 23. Open weekends only February and March. Closed Thanksgiving, Christmas, and during January.

Directions: From **I-95,** take the Thornburg exit. Go west on Rte. 606 for 2.5 miles and cross the intersection at Snell to Rte. 208. Go 11.5 miles on Rte. 208 to the winery entrance, on the left.

Phone: 540-895-5085
Fax: 540-895-9749
E-mail: lakeannawinery@cs.com
Website: www.lawinery.com

Tasting fee: None to taste any 4 wines; for more than 4, $2 per person

Wines: Cabernet Sauvignon, Merlot, Chardonnay, Seyval Blanc, *Spotsylvania Claret, Lake Side Red, Lake Side White*

Wine related items for sale? Yes
Picnic area? Yes
Facilities for private functions? Yes

Owners: Bill and Ann Heidig, with sons Eric and Jeff Heidig
Winemaker: Bill Heidig

Bill Heidig admits there was a time when he didn't care very much for wine. It wasn't until he found himself traveling abroad at least once a month in his Defense Department job that he began first to sample and then to enjoy fine European wines. The fact that when in Europe he usually drank it as an accompaniment to food probably had a lot to do with the rapid development of his appreciation for good wine—and before long for the notion that he might like to grow grapes on his farm in Spotsylvania County.

Bill had become disenchanted with the traditional crops he was raising. "In fact," he says, "if you look at the price of corn or soybeans today, it's the same as it was twenty years ago." In 1983 after consulting with Jim Law, who now owns Linden Vineyards, Bill and his wife, Ann, and other family members, set out 2,000 Seyval Blanc vines. They used a rented tree planter pulled behind a tractor, and as the equipment moved along punching deep holes in the earth, human hands dropped the vines into the holes. Later, the tree planter became unavailable, and vine planting technology in Bill's vineyards reverted to the use of a subsoiler to get below the hardpan and a wedge-shaped shovel called a dibble. Inserted into the loose ground and rocked back and forth, the dibble creates funnel-shaped holes for accepting the new vines. Nearly all of the Heidigs' twenty-three acres of grapes have been planted this way.

It's generally accepted, Bill says, that while other winegrowing regions in this country are producing vintages of great distinction and quality, Virginia wines are closer in style to those you'll find in Europe. This is not surprising, since the soils and microclimates in the state bear strong resemblances to those found in Europe. Wine judges and wine critics are bestowing world-class designations on Virginia-made wines with accelerating frequency, and Bill gives much of the credit for the recent surge in the quality of Virginia wines to improved vineyard practices. The people most responsible for that are those involved in the state's viticultural program, certainly one of the best anywhere in the country.

Knowing when to pick the fruit seems elementary, but according to Bill, in the early years of Virginia's renascent winegrowing industry, he and many other growers were harvesting the grapes too soon, not giving them time to produce sufficient sugars or fully develop their specific varietal virtues. Good canopy management, something he learned through the extension program, means accurately assessing the best time and the best spot for leaf pulling so the grapes will get just the right amount of exposure to the sun.

Crop thinning is essential to producing good quality fruit, the only thing from which a winemaker can make good quality wine. "Basically what you're looking for," says Bill, "is a balance between the fruit that you're growing and the root structure that's providing the nutrients for that growth. You have to figure out where that delicate balance is for a particular plant—whether the roots are sufficiently developed to allow the plant to have more fruit or not. Some varieties—Seyval, for example—will produce a tremendous crop. You have to remove some of it so that the quality of that vintage won't be compromised." Growing grapes clearly is not like growing corn, where the farmer is trying to get as many ears from the stalk as he possibly can.

It's important to get *some* fruit off the vines, though, so weather conditions at the time of bud break are critical. The buds—which start off as single leaves—give rise to shoots, some of which will bear fruit, and are actually three buds in one. A fruit-bearing shoot from a primary bud will produce at least two clusters of fruit. If anything happens to it—a late spring frost is its number one enemy—the secondary bud erupts, but its shoot produces a single cluster at most. If *it* dies, the tertiary bud will open—but its shoot bears nothing except leaves. Fruit trees, Bill notes, do the same thing. Some years peach trees or apple trees won't have any fruit at all because both the primary and secondary buds were somehow destroyed.

Lake Anna's wine list is tailored to appeal specifically to the tastes of two factions: Bill Heidig and Bill Heidig's customers. The winemaker himself prefers dry wines and observes that as people allow themselves to sample more wines at the drier end of the spectrum, their palates tend to dry out as well. For those for whom wine appreciation is in its early stages, sweeter wines are often more appealing, and with varying degrees of sweetness, they definitely have their place paired with spicier dishes and desserts or as aperitifs and after-dinner drinks. There are several ways to make semi-dry and sweet wines. Sugar or unfermented juice can be added to a dry, finished wine, which is then filtered to remove any yeast that could convert the new sugar to alcohol. Residual sugar results when the fermentation process is intentionally halted—usually by dropping the temperature below thirty degrees Fahrenheit—before all the sugar has been converted.

The Heidig's winery is located three miles from Lake Anna and eighteen miles from Fredericksburg. During the War Between the States, four major battles were fought in or around this town, strategically located midway between Washington and Richmond. Bill was never a Civil War enthusiast until he got the idea of featuring the local battles on the labels for his *Spotsylvania Claret,* one of Lake Anna's most popular wines. Reading the labels, you'll find out about the surprising decision reached by Robert E. Lee and Stonewall Jackson regarding troop deployment at the Battle of Chancellorsville. At Bloody Angle, Confederate soldiers fighting the Battle of Spotsylvania Courthouse paid a high price for ignoring standard military practice.

By the time you leave this winery you'll have learned a little Civil War history and sampled some excellent wines—both with the compliments of an award-winning winemaker who at one time wasn't particularly interested in either.

The Williamsburg Winery

The Williamsburg Winery
and Gabriel Archer Tavern
5800 Wessex Hundred
Williamsburg, VA 23185

Hours: 10 a.m. to 5:30 p.m. Monday through Saturday; noon to 5:30 p.m. on Sunday.

Directions: From **Rte. 199**, turn onto Brookwood Drive, then left onto Lake Powell Road and go 1 mile to winery entrance. From **Richmond** via I-64, take exit 234 to Rte. 199 east. From **Newport News** via I-64, take exit 242A to Rte. 199 west. From **Colonial Williamsburg**, take Rte. 132 south (S. Henry Street) and turn right onto Rte. 199.

Phone: 757-229-0999
Fax: 757-229-0911
E-mail: wine@wmbgwine.com
Website: www.williamsburg-wineryltd.com

Tasting fee: Small tasting fee includes guided tour of largest barrel cellar in Virginia and engraved souvenir glass.

Wines: Cabernets, Merlots, Chardonnays, reserves, dessert wines, *Governor's White, Two Shilling Red, James River White, Plantation Blush, Gabriel Archer Reserve*

Wine related items for sale? Yes
Food available? Light luncheon fare at the Gabriel Archer Tavern
Special Programs? Virginia Tastevin Society
Facilities for private functions? Yes

Owners: the Duffeler family and associates
Winemaker: Steve Warner
Viticulturist: Ben Tomes

History seems to be at the task of making amends, having located the state's largest winery where 400 years ago the first wine-drinking people to settle here tried repeatedly—and failed consistently—to grow European grapes on Virginia soil.

The 320 acres of Wessex Hundred Farm are on land picked out by Gabriel Archer, co-pilot of the sailing vessel the *Godspeed,* as the best site for the first permanent English settlement in the New World. Archer's recommendation lost out to that of Captain John Smith, who chose an island two miles farther north on the James River. Twelve years after Jamestown was settled in April of 1607, the first House of Burgesses convened to enact legislation appropriate to the safety and success of the colony and the furtherance of the commercial aims of the settlement's sponsors, the Virginia Company of London. Acte Twelfth of Sixteen Nineteen required that every householder plant—each year—ten vines for the purpose of growing and making wine.

When Patrick and Peggy Duffeler bought the property in 1983, they were not aware of the historical significance of the farm; they were simply looking for a suitable piece of land on which to start a vineyard and winery. Patrick had visited Williamsburg in 1961 as an exchange student from Belgium and been taken with the history and charm of Virginia's restored colonial capital. After searching the state over, the Duffelers decided on the Williamsburg property.

With a master's degree in economics and close to twenty years' experience in international marketing, Patrick came to Virginia well equipped to own and operate a business the size of the Williamsburg Winery. In 1971 his entrepreneurial approach to marketing and his talent for getting things done had landed him the assignment of building a Formula 1 racing team from the ground up for Philip Morris. The Marlboro team soon dominated the world of sports car racing, and during the five years that he managed the team, Patrick attended every Grand Prix in the world—but he never drove a Formula 1 car.

Likewise the owner of Virginia's largest winery has never himself made any wine. "I can assure you of one thing," he says, "I have drunk a fair amount of wine in my lifetime. I have always been interested," he adds, "in watching, in learning, in understanding. Everybody's got his profession. Mine is not winemaking. That's why I have a top winemaker here. In nearly fifteen years of working together, I have never overturned a decision that Steve Warner has made."

In 1984 Steve graduated from Fresno State University with a master's degree in enology. He immediately stunned family and friends by announcing that he was leaving California, the largest wine producing region in the Americas, to go make wine in Virginia. After three years at two other Virginia wineries, he was hired by the Duffelers in time for their first crush in 1987. The first vines at Williamsburg had been planted in 1985, and as yet the winery didn't have any grapes of its own to process. But Patrick was eager to get started. With 100 percent purchased fruit, Steve produced 2,500 cases of wine. From then on expansion at Williamsburg was by leaps and bounds.

An intransigent distaste for the wines made from hardy native grapes and the divers unrelenting assaults of a harsh new environment on the relatively fragile European vines eventually depleted the winegrowing enthusiasm of Virginia's early settlers. In 1776, after previously extolling York County as eminently suited to the purpose, the General Assembly threw up their hands in frustration and declared the Williamsburg environs manifestly unfit for growing grapes. Today there are sixty acres of grafted vinifera—Cabernet Sauvignon, Merlot, and Chardonnay—thriving at the Williamsburg site. The winery owns another eleven acres of hybrid vines at Dominion Wine Cellars, a former co-op venture which they acquired in 1993. This combined acreage is not enough to meet the needs of Williamsburg, which currently produces 70,000 cases a year and has 100,000 cases in the cross hairs of its short term plans. The winery gets most of the rest of its grapes from vineyards it owns or leases throughout the commonwealth.

Arriving at the winery after a visit to historic Williamsburg, you get the impression that a portion of Duke of Gloucester Street has been lifted from its foundations and set down amid the vineyards. The architectural elements of mixed brick and lap siding, steeply pitched, cedar shake roofs, and dormer windows all proclaim Colonial Williamsburg. There's the Early American look of private dwellings happily sharing the street front with small businesses, in nearly equal proportions. Entrance to the winery is through the retail shop and browsing is as welcome and rewarding here as it is downtown.

The wine list at Williamsburg is extensive and reads in part like a lesson in the general and viticultural history of Virginia. *Acte 12 of 1619 Chardonnay* is barrel aged in French oak and remembers the efforts of the early colonial representatives to encourage a winemaking industry. *John Adlum Chardonnay* pays tribute to a fellow surveyor and friend of George Washington who gained renown as a horticulturist and viticultural advisor to Thomas Jefferson. The *Gabriel Archer Reserve* blend of Cabernet Sauvignon, Cabernet Franc, and Merlot toasts the man who thought the land that now surrounds the winery was the safest place for those aboard the *Godspeed,* the *Susan Constant,* and the *Discovery* to disembark.

Full suits of armor stand guard in Wessex Hall, one of two "great halls" which are used by the winery for special events and are also available for private functions. Long, unvarnished wooden floor planks stretch the perspective in these European-style gathering rooms, where Old World curiosities like jousting sticks, Spanish swords, and conquistador helmets take you back several centuries. The museum

The Williamsburg Winery

at the winery houses colonial-era artifacts found on the property, as well as Patrick's extensive collection of eighteenth-century onion-shaped wine bottles from a plantation in South America.

While taking the tour at Williamsburg, you'll also get a peek at the bottling line and a bird's eye view of the largest stainless steel tank at any Virginia winery. This gargantuan vessel holds 4,800 cases. If you and a friend were to share a bottle of its wine every single day, it would take you 165 *years* to empty the 12,000-gallon tank. You could start with a glass apiece at the Gabriel Archer Tavern after you've finished the tour. Visitors can order their favorite Williamsburg wines and a light lunch, to be savored inside or enjoyed outside on the brick-paved terrace in front of the tavern—or the one in back next to the vines.

At Williamsburg they feel passionately about Virginia's future as a major wine producing state. Patrick believes Virginia wines will be mainly regional for the next ten years; the industry still hasn't completely conquered its own local market. The ultimate success of winegrowers in the state will depend on keeping a sharp eye on consumer patterns, like the current rapid shift from white to red wine consumption among Americans. Spotting and even forecasting trends is important because grape growing, as Patrick points out, is very much a futures game. Vines ordered one year and planted the next will not yield a good, economic harvest for three or four more years. To these, add eighteen months in the barrels and another two years of bottle aging for a premium wine and the period between investment and return on investment stretches to nearly a decade.

Four centuries ago the first Virginians invested their hopes and their labors to prove what seemed obvious: that this new place on earth was ideally outfitted for producing wines to compete with those of the established grape growing regions of Europe. A more recent newcomer to Virginia's shores is succeeding where the earliest settlers, through no fault of their own, could not. With the founding of the Williamsburg Winery, the history of winemaking in Virginia has come full circle—but with a happy ending. As for the state's winemaking future—since starting his small winery where grape growing was first attempted in Virginia, Patrick's motto has always been "The best is yet to come."

69

Windy River Winery

Windy River Winery
20268 Teman Road
Beaverdam, VA 23015

Hours: Noon to 5 p.m. on Saturday and 1 p.m. to 5 p.m. on Sunday during February and March. Noon to 5 p.m. Thursday through Saturday and 1 p.m. to 5 p.m. on Sunday from April through December.

Directions: From **I-95 northbound,** take exit 98 (Doswell). Turn left onto Rte. 30, then right onto U.S. Rte. 1 north. At Rte. 684, turn left. Go 10 miles to Rte. 738. Turn right (Teman Road) and go 1.5 miles to the winery, on the right. From **I-95 southbound,** take exit 110 (Ladysmith). Turn right onto Rte. 639 and go 6 miles to Rte. 738 (Anderson Mill Road) in Chilesburg. Turn left onto Rte. 738 and go 4 miles to the winery, on the left.

Phone: 804-449-6996
Fax: 804-449-6138
E-mail: kathryn@windyriverwinery.com
Website: www.windyriverwinery.com

Tasting fee: None

Wines: Cabernet Sauvignon, Merlot, Chardonnay, Viognier, Cayuga, *The Wolf, Wolf Blanc, Roué*

Wine related items for sale? Yes
Picnic area? Yes
Food available? Light snacks
Facilities for private functions? Yes

Owners: Judith and Kathryn Rocchiccioli
Winemaker: Judith Rocchiccioli
Viticulturist: Kathryn Rocchiccioli

Rural Virginia of a hundred years ago is typified in this white frame farmhouse perched serenely atop a hill in historic Hanover County. Randy and Judith Rocchiccioli purchased Windy River Farm in 1991 and immediately set about remodeling the old house and, in 1993, planting their first vines. The sprawling front porch of the house, which once presented fields of traditional southern crops, now presides over twelve acres of vinifera grapes, including Merlot, Cabernet Sauvignon, Chardonnay, Cabernet Franc, Viognier, and Pinot Noir. Winemaker Judith has taken care to preserve the bygone charm of this two-over-two country dwelling, whose sitting room, adjacent to the first-floor tasting room, is filled with rustic antique furniture.

Winemaking is a tradition with the Rocchicciolis. Randy's grandfather was a winegrower in Tuscany, and his family still cultivates vineyards in Italy. A brother runs a West Coast start-up version of Rocchiccioli Vineyards in California's Napa Valley. Here at Windy River, daughter-in-law Kathryn assists with the winemaking and has responsibility for the vineyards, as well as for the day-to-day operations of the winery.

Judith got her start making wine at home for the family and has augmented her extensive self-education with courses at U.C. Davis, the winemaking campus in California. As you sip a glass of her award-winning *Wolf Blanc,* a blend of Seyval and Muscat, you'll notice the subtle hint of apple and apricot, fruity essences imparted by the grapes themselves. The yeast plays a role in eliciting these copycat flavors. Judith, whose background is in research for healthcare services, now concentrates on yeast research. By blending different types of yeast she is able to coax a variety of flavors from the grapes. Wine production at Windy River runs the gamut from the

Beaujolais nouveau method of bottling the wine when it is still quite young to cold fermenting in stainless steel tanks to extended aging in French or American oak barrels.

To most people wine is synonymous with the good life, and for the owners of Windy River the good life means friends and lots of them. Their love of people is reflected in their love of music and entertainment, which they share throughout the warmer months by hosting music festivals and outdoor theatrical performances. Jazz and bluegrass concerts alternate with Shakespeare and Oscar Wilde in the winery's pavilion, earning rave reviews for the performers and thanks from local groups who are often the beneficiaries of these events.

This winery enjoys an unmistakable identity for its brand in the Windy River Lady, the chic and slender beauty variously depicted on their labels. Original art for the labels hangs in the tasting and sitting rooms at the farmhouse, and a case purchase will get you a free copy. Though their marketing efforts are currently concentrated in Virginia, they are licensed to ship out of state, and the Windy River label circulates world wide. Aficionados as far away as Australia and Japan who have received gifts of *Wolf* (named for a blue-eyed Siberian husky) or *Roué,* Windy River's "wine of passion," regularly e-mail their thoughts of appreciation.

Windy River is a small winery encompassed by some very large history. Only a few miles away is Scotchtown, home of Revolutionary firebrand Patrick Henry. Closer still is North Anna Battlefield Park. During the Civil War the usually calm North Anna River flowed nervously between two opposing armies, while thirty miles away Richmond held its breath. The quiet setting belies the history of the property, whose gently rolling hills once shuddered in the rumble of North/South artillery exchange. At a farm near Beaverdam Station, a young Confederate officer named John Singleton Mosby, soon to become the legendary Gray Ghost, somehow managed to get himself captured—though not for long.

Speaking of ghosts, if you're seated on the back row at one of this winery's open-air performances and feel something brush softly across your shoulders, turn around slowly. You may have just had a close encounter with the other Windy River Lady. Staff members have reported sightings in the vineyard, in the lane in front of the Rocchicciolis' house, and in the winery's front yard. No relation to the lass on the winery's label, this Windy River Lady has been making brief appearances in the Beaverdam area for years, but she seems especially interested in the new goings-on at the winery. Her bona fide reputation has led L.B. Taylor, Jr., author of the popular *Ghosts of Virginia* series, to devote an entire chapter to her in his upcoming *Volume V.*

Breaux Vineyards

Breaux Vineyards
36888 Breaux Vineyards Lane
Hillsboro, VA 20132

Hours: Open daily 11 a.m. to 5 p.m. from November through April and 11 a.m. to 6 p.m. from May through October. Closed New Year's Day, Easter, July 4th, Thanksgiving, and Christmas. Call for hours on other holidays.

Directions: From **northern Virginia,** take Dulles Toll Road west (Rte. 267) to Greenway. At Leesburg, take Rte. 7 west 3 miles to Rte. 9 west. Go 8 miles to Hillsboro, then another 1.5 miles to Rte. 671 (Harper's Ferry Road). Bear right on Rte. 671 and continue 1 mile to winery, on the right. From **Maryland,** take Rte. 340 to Rte. 671 and go 7 miles to winery, on the left.

Phone: 540-668-6299
Fax: 540-668-6283
E-mail: breauxvin@aol.com
Website: www.breauxvineyards.com

Tasting fee: None, except $3 per person for groups of 8 or more

Wines: Chardonnay, Viognier, Sauvignon Blanc, Seyval Blanc, Vidal Blanc, Cabernet Sauvignon, Merlot

Wine related items for sale? Yes
Picnic area? Yes
Food available? Light snacks
Facilities for private functions? Yes

Owners: Paul and Alexis Breaux
Winemaker: David Collins

The cool leaf of a grapevine gently pressed against the vineyardist's cheek not only provides a moment's relief on a hot summer day, it tells something about the health of the vine. Plants transpire, giving off moisture to keep their temperature down when the atmosphere heats up, along with oxygen for us to breathe. A leaf from a vine that is diseased or overly stressed for water will be noticeably warmer than the foliage on a healthy vine whose roots are getting all the moisture they need from deep—sometimes thirty or forty feet deep—in the earth.

When a European variety of grapevine is first planted, care must be taken not to cover the graft joint with soil. Otherwise, the plant will try to root from the upper, fruit-bearing (or scion) portion and possibly fall victim to disease and pests—such as phylloxera—that would not affect its hardier American rootstock base.

These are things about grape growing that Paul Breaux might never have known if he had not bought his 400-acre farm in Loudoun County in 1994 as a place to semi-retire from his real estate business and, in his words, "to hide from the world." The property came with 2½ acres of abandoned Chardonnay, Cabernet Sauvignon, and Seyval vines that had become completely overgrown in tall grass and scrub. The vines had been planted a decade earlier by local winemaker David Collins, who had once worked for the farm's former owners.

Paul and his wife, Alexis, enlisted David's help in identifying the varieties and restoring the vineyard. In 1996, under David's guidance, the Breaux used the grapes from their reclaimed vines to vint homemade wine, which they later shared at a party attended by over 100 guests. David was there and witnessed the enthusiasm expressed for the Breaux's first vintage. Before long he presented Paul with a business plan for starting a vineyard and winery. Breaux Vineyards now has forty-three acres in vines and produces 10,000 cases of wine a year, some of it coming out of the original vineyard.

The original winery was in a corrugated-metal building which Paul built when his intentions were simply to become a gentleman farmer. The tasting room opened in 1998 in what was to have been the farm manager's office. It has been transformed by Alexis into a beautifully appointed salon for sampling David Collins's award-winning wines, some of which are displayed in a softly lit ambry at the back of the room. Rough-plastered surfaces the color of beach grass recall warm, sunlit walls in the south of France. Arched windows and Italian floor tiles in blended shades of gold, green, and brown create a relaxed, Mediterranean mood that is easily sustained outside on the stone-paved terrace. On Patio Madeleine, named for the Breaux's daughter, you can enjoy gourmet cheeses and patés, along with French breads baked by a French woman, and your favorite Breaux wines.

Paul is a Louisiana Cajun by way of California and North Carolina, and his Gulf State heritage is symbolized on the winery's label in the form of the crawfish, a backwater delicacy and cousin of the shrimp. Breaux's *Lafayette,* a blend of Cabernet Franc and Cabernet Sauvignon, is named not for the French champion of the American Revolution but for Lafayette, Louisiana, which *was* no doubt named for the much-honored marquis and is the center of Cajun culture.

Evangeline—a proprietary blend of white grape varieties—celebrates the heroine of Henry Wadsworth Longfellow's epic poem about the migration of the French-speaking Acadians from Canada to Louisiana. There's even a bit of the bayou in the tank room, where wary alligators all but entirely submerged beneath the concrete floor train patient, reptilian eyes on unwary winery visitors.

In 1999, Breaux doubled the size of its production area and raised the roof on the winery to accommodate new stainless steel tanks imported from Germany. Within the very near future they will add a stone-encased barrel cellar, which will be used not only for aging their wines but for special events such as winemaker dinners. After that, a new, larger tasting room will be constructed, and the current tasting room will be available for private functions. The architectural style of the existing hospitality area will be carried forward in these next phases of expansion.

All these changes, and more, have become necessary to accommodate the steadily increasing flow of visitors to the winery—people who are looking for exceptional Virginia wines they can enjoy amid splendid rural Virginia surroundings. The world has discovered Paul Breaux's hiding place, but the gregarious and hospitable Cajun doesn't seem to mind at all.

Farfelu Vineyards & Winery

Farfelu Vineyards & Winery
13058 Crest Hill Road
Flint Hill, VA 22627

Hours: Noon until 4:30 p.m. Saturday and Sunday from April through November.

Directions: From **D.C.,** take I-66 west to the second Marshall exit (exit 27). At the top of the exit ramp, turn left, crossing over the highway. Turn right onto Crest Hill Road (Rte. 647) and go 12 miles to the winery entrance, on the left. From **Charlottesville,** take Rte. 29 north to Warrenton. Take Rte. 211 west for 4.5 miles and turn right onto Route 688. Go 9 miles and turn left onto Rte. 647. Go 3.5 miles to the winery, on the left.

Phone: 540-364-2930
E-mail: c-osborne@farfeluwine.com
Website: www.farfeluwine.com

Tasting fee: None

Wines: Cabernet Sauvignon, Chardonnay, *Fou de Blanc, Fou de Rouge*

Wine related items for sale? Yes
Picnic area? Yes
Food available? Light snacks
Facilities for private functions? Yes

Owners: John and Caroline Osborne
Winemaker: Caroline Osborne
Consulting Winemaker: Chris Pearmund
Viticulturist: Jim Furr

While exploring Virginia wine country, you'll discover quite a few barns that have been pressed into winemaking service, but you won't find any more interesting or picturesque than this 130-year-old hill barn at Farfelu Vineyards. Hill, or bank, barns are just what their name implies. They are built into the side of a hill to take advantage of the insulating effect of the surrounding earth. According to winery founder Chuck Raney, this structure was probably at one time a dairy barn, and the hillside walls, with their fieldstone facing, kept the inside a little cooler in summer and a little warmer in winter. These days the winery and barrel room benefit from the underground construction.

The corncrib was built directly overtop the barn. Air circulation is mandatory in a corncrib in order for the grain to dry out and keep over the winter months. Livestock love corn on the cob and don't seem to mind that the kernels get as hard as brick in places like this, where sunlight and wind currents stream through chinks in the loosely spaced vertical siding. A trap door in the floor allowed the farmer to drop feed to his animals below. When it came time to start making wine, Chuck had a ready-made gravity-flow system for his winery. The former corncrib, which has a new steel-reinforced concrete floor, is now the crush pad. Grapes from Farfelu's vineyards are brought over the hill and into the crib. The crusher/destemmer is placed over the trap door, and the crushed white grapes are funneled directly into the press below. The must of red grapes goes into fermentation vats, which are rolled under the opening on dollies.

Farfelu is probably the oldest continuously cultivated vineyard in Virginia. Chuck planted his first vines in 1967, a year after buying the eighty-six-acre parcel in Rappahannock County. There were virtually no wineries operating in the state at the time, so his plan was to sell the grapes to home winemakers and use the profits to expand the vineyard and ultimately fund his winery. In 1975, while still working full time as a commercial airline pilot, Chuck applied for and received his winery license.

In the year 2000, the silver anniversary of his commercial winemaking career, Chuck retired from the business and turned the operation of Farfelu Vineyards over to new owners John and Caroline Osborne. This winery started small and has remained small by design. Chuck and his wife, Virginia, bottled under 400 cases of wine a year. The Osbornes will be expanding and expect to more than double production—to 1,000 cases—their first year. They are planting more vines and while waiting for these to mature, will buy grapes from other Virginia growers. Caroline is the winemaker, working with and learning from Chris Pearmund, one of the state's most accomplished winemakers and winegrowers.

Chuck Raney's experimental planting of 110 vines in 1967 included eleven varieties. Today Farfelu Vineyards is growing a mix of vinifera (Cabernet Sauvignon, Merlot, Syrah, Mourvedre, and Chardonnay) and French hybrids Chancellor and De Chaunac, as well as the American hybrid Cayuga. There are currently four wines for sampling—two whites and two reds. The Chardonnay is barrel fermented in French oak. The Cayuga—which the Osbornes are calling *Fou de Blanc,* or "crazy little white"—is a semi-dry picnic wine with less than 2 percent residual sugar and is fermented in stainless steel. Red wine lovers will appreciate Farfelu's softly tannic Cabernet Sauvignon and may even go a little crazy for *Fou de Rouge,* a dry picnic blend of Chancellor and De Chaunac. Caroline's first addition to Farfelu's family of wines will marry Bordeaux and the Rhone Valley in a blend of Cabernet Franc and Syrah.

The elevation at Farfelu is around 500 feet. Vineyards, like corncribs, need air circulation to keep the fruit dry and free from mildew and rot. Water acts as a conduit, drawing cooler air towards it. The Rappahannock River runs through the property, pulling a draft through the vines, helping to keep the grape clusters dry during the hot, humid Virginia summers. People are also drawn to the Rappahannock, one of the cleanest, most scenic rivers in the state. If you visit the winery on a sultry day, you'll find there's a cool breeze stirring on the hiking trail down by the river.

About fifty years ago a row of horse stalls was added to the dairy barn. An overhang from one end of the addition to the other creates a rustic colonnade effect, with each of the ten stalls opening to the outside. The siding on the barn has weathered to a random pattern of silvers and bronzes. Inside, arched doors from a church soften the architectural edges, adding to the already considerable charm of this antique structure. The tasting room is right next to the original barn in what was once the groom's room. Whenever a mare was about to foal, the groom would stay here overnight. The two stalls adjacent to his room were for expectant equine mothers. The winemaker's lab now occupies one of them, and the equipment room is in the other.

Chuck Raney was reading an English version of an André Malraux novel when he first encountered the French word *farfelu.* It's not easy trying to pin down the precise meaning of this archaic adjective. Even Malraux's translator felt more comfortable leaving it in the original French. *Screwy* or *a little bit nuts* are fair approximations and accurately describe how many people viewed Chuck's venture into winegrowing in Virginia during the late sixties. Given the longevity of Farfelu's vineyards and the tremendous success of the state's new grape growing industry, it wasn't such a crazy idea after all.

Gray Ghost Winery

Gray Ghost Winery
14706 Lee Highway
Amissville, VA 20106

Hours: 11 a.m. to 5 p.m. Saturday and Sunday during January and February; Friday, Saturday, and Sunday from March through December; as well as all Monday federal holidays. Closed Easter, Christmas, and New Year's Day.

Directions: From **D.C. area,** take I-66 west to Rte. 29 south. Take Rte. 211 west (Warrenton exit) and go 11 miles. Winery is on the left side of divided highway. From **Richmond,** take I-95 north to Rte. 17 north to Rte. 29 north. Take first Warrenton exit (business Rte. 29). Take left exit to Rte. 211 west and go 11 miles to winery, on left of divided highway.

Phone: 540-937-4869
Fax: 540-937-4869

Tasting fee: None, except small charge for limited release wines

Wines: Cabernet Sauvignon, Cabernet Franc, Merlot, Chardonnay, Seyval Blanc, Vidal Blanc, *Victorian Red, Victorian White, Adieu*

Wine related items for sale? Yes
Picnic area? Yes
Food available? Light snacks
Facilities for private functions? Yes

Owners: Al and Cheryl Kellert
Winemakers/Viticulturists: Al and Cheryl Kellert

As far as we know, John Singleton Mosby himself never penned the term *Gray Ghost*. He did, however, pen every letter that makes up the nickname by which he was known to the Union troops whose camps and supply lines he raided on a near nightly basis. Al and Cheryl Kellert are avid collectors of Civil War and Mosby memorabilia. The very authentic looking signature that appears on their winery's label was lifted, character by character, from letters they have acquired that were indeed authored by the Confederate colonel.

The winery is located in Amissville, which is at the southern end of what was referred to in his day as Mosby's Confederacy. Al can precisely define that territory for you, where the elusive colonel would, as he puts it, "spend his time harassing General Grant." When the war was over, Al is quick to point out, the two former enemies became close personal friends. The Kellerts, who are originally from the Midwest, are enthusiastic transplants to Virginia soil. There's a cavalry saber hanging on the wall in the tasting room, which is starting to take on the character of a small museum. Says Al with the zeal of the dedicated collector, "We are trying our best to get the Southern Civil War weapons back into the South." This particular example of Confederate weaponry was repatriated from Ohio.

There's a portrait, an original oil painting from a photograph taken at the beginning of the war, that is Cheryl's favorite picture of John Mosby. Ladies, be advised, this is not the bearded, war-worn visage of the Gray Ghost you're used to seeing. To be plain about it, the colonel was a handsome man.

But they do other things at Gray Ghost besides steep themselves in Civil War history. They're also making wines the likes of which the average Union or Confederate soldier never had the pleasure of tasting. They don't crush any of their grapes, including the reds. Instead Al and Cheryl use a special piece of equipment that gently knocks the fruit off the stems and breaks the skins. The grapes are then slowly pumped into the tanks for fermenting, in the case of the reds, or into the press, in the case of the whites. The equipment is like a crusher/destemmer without the crusher, and the process can be loosely compared to the whole-cluster pressing of white grapes employed by many winemakers.

The Kellerts have eleven acres of vines from which they get roughly two-thirds of their fruit. Their reserve Chardonnay, an international award winner in 1997, is 100 percent estate grown. Cheryl manages the vineyards, and her objective "is that the vines have to be absolutely perfect, which means the fruit comes in absolutely perfect." *Reserve* is a term whose criteria vary from season to season and winemaker to winemaker. Gray Ghost's reserve Cabernet Sauvignon is produced only in a year with an impeccable growing season—1998, for example—and is a pure varietal. After fermentation a mere three barrels of free-run juice—wine collected before it is pressed off the skins—is immediately put into French oak where it ages for three years and goes through malolactic fermentation to soften the acids.

Other varietals at Gray Ghost include a 100 percent Seyval fermented in French oak. Their Cabernet Franc is also unblended, while their nonreserve Cabernet Sauvignon is softened with a little Franc and Merlot. *Victorian Red* is an interesting combining of Cabernet Franc and Chardonnay designed by the Kellerts to help white wine drinkers transition to the pleasures of red wine, and it serves its purpose very well.

Getting back to the war—at the end of it John Mosby, rather than surrender, simply disbanded his unit in an address whose last words were "and I bid you a final adieu." With almost poignant double meaning, Al and Cheryl have named their late harvest Vidal—the season's farewell grape—*Adieu*. With over 11 percent residual sugar, this wine reminds you that while parting may indeed be sorrow, it can also be very, very sweet.

The Kellerts' winery is a family enterprise which employs daughter Amy Payette in a marketing capacity and son Al on a part-time basis and produces about 3,000 cases a year. The owners want to grow, but not to the point that they lose the close relationships they have developed with their clientele. There's a strong reciprocal loyalty for the winery, too. One customer, while in California, went so far as to hang a sign on the Napa Valley wine train pointing the way to Gray Ghost Winery—"2,985 miles east."

The barrels and stainless steel tanks once shared the same quarters in the winery, an area as neat as a barracks which you can see through the french doors in the tasting room. The Kellerts have recently constructed a three-story building that stretches across the far end of the Victorian Garden and houses the underground barrel room and wine library. Skyrocket junipers will eventually enclose the garden, creating an intimate space for visitors to relax, have a picnic, and maybe sip a little wine.

Gray Ghost is a popular destination for tours organized by a number of historical societies. Since 1995 the Kellerts have hosted an annual authors' weekend at the winery. This increasingly popular event, which takes place in November, initially attracted only eight writers, who came to talk to people about their books. The two-day affair recently brought together more than twenty-five authors from North and South who have written on the Kellerts' favorite nonviticultural subject, the War Between the States.

When Al and Cheryl decided to look for a place to start a vineyard, they wanted to be sure to pick a spot that was easily accessible. Their location right on Route 211 fit the bill perfectly. You can't miss it. But if you do, simply make a left at the next crossover and double back to what is sure to be one of your favorite stops on the Virginia winery tour.

Hartwood Winery

Hartwood Winery
345 Hartwood Road
Fredericksburg, VA 22406

Hours: 11 a.m. to 5 p.m. Wednesday through Friday; 11 a.m. to 6 p.m. Saturday and Sunday. Closed Thanksgiving, Christmas, and New Year's Day.

Directions: From the intersection of Rtes. 17 and 95 at **Fredericksburg,** go 6 miles north on Rte. 17 and turn right onto Rte. 612. Go 2 miles to the winery, on the left.

Phone: 540-752-4893
Fax: 540-752-4893
E-mail: jdliving@erols.com

Tasting fee: None, except $3 per person for groups of 20 or more

Wines: Cabernet Sauvignon, Chambourcin, Chardonnay, Seyval Blanc, Vidal Blanc, *Rappahannock Red, Rappahannock White*

Wine related items for sale? Yes
Picnic area? Yes
Food available? Light snacks
Special Programs? Wine appreciation classes
Facilities for private functions? Yes

Owners: Jim and Beverly Livingston
Winemakers/Viticulturists: Jim and Beverly Livingston

This winery is a perfect example of how to get into the business incrementally with a little help from your friends. In 1970, when he was fresh out of graduate school, Jim Livingston joined a wine tasting society in Fredericksburg. When the club's founder announced she was going to do the then unthinkable and try her own hand at growing wine grapes, he immediately volunteered to help plant them. No sooner were Lucie Morton's vines in the ground at a farm in King George County than Jim decided to plant a few of his own. Back home in Fredericksburg he set out ten or fifteen vines in his backyard.

A few years later a friend with a little land to spare offered him the use of an acre. "I planted several different varieties," Jim says, "just to see what they would do." At the time everything he read about grape growing in the state told him that, as far as what would grow well here, Virginia was a vast unknown. Before long the one acre had become two and then four. At the end of five years there were seven varieties—until Jim decided to uproot four of them. When asked why, he responds matter-of-factly, "They didn't make good wine."

In the mid-eighties, Jim sold property he owned on Lake Anna in Spotsylvania County in order to buy the fifteen acres on which Hartwood Winery is located. The vineyards were established in 1984 and 1985. There are seven acres of French hybrids—Vidal, Seyval, and Chambourcin—at the winery site. Hartwood controls other acreage on which they grow their vinifera, including Chardonnay and Cabernet Sauvignon.

The winery is on land that was once part of an immense tract owned by an Englishman. In his day the deer were so plentiful that he named his farm for the antlered species. The area around it became known as Hartwood as well. As Jim recounts it, the gentleman once wrote home noting, "I do not starve, for I have plenty of hart." In recent years agriculture throughout Virginia, including vineyards like Jim's, has been experiencing extreme deer pressure. So severe, in fact, that if the Englishman were a winegrower in Virginia today, he might write home that the hart are not starving, for they have plenty of grapes.

Inside the tasting room there are so many hart they occasionally get underfoot. There's a wooden plaque on the wall

behind the bar bearing the winery's deer and grape-cluster motif. It was designed by Jim's sister-in-law, who also rendered the seven-point stag on the floor. A friend then used a blowtorch to burn the image into the wooden planks. The lumber for the bar and the floor, and most of the rest of the winery, came right off the property. Friends helped cut down the trees, which Jim had milled to his specifications. Less than six months later, with friends pitching in on weekends, Jim had built his winery. It opened in June of 1989.

David Barber is a partner at Hartwood, and on weekends he can be found either helping Jim and his wife, Beverly, in the winery or behind the bar helping customers understand and fully appreciate the wine experience. David, who is a certified wine judge, teaches wine classes at the winery, and during the tasting you can get a short course in, for example, the difference between the terms *aroma* and *bouquet*.

Aromas are discrete sensory perceptions that come from the grapes themselves. A Cabernet may impart, among others, the aroma of cherries; a Chardonnay, those of apples and pears. The bouquet is the entire olfactory experience you enjoy with a particular wine. It includes the aromas from the grape—or grapes if it's a blend—as well as other things, like the spiciness of the oak and the nuances derived from malolactic fermentation. A bouquet can be fruity, or herbaceous, or floral—or a combination of these or other descriptors you may devise yourself to express the overall sensation of extreme pleasure arriving at your brain via your nose. As David will tell you, appreciation of its bouquet is at least half the enjoyment of a good wine.

"Every time you age a wine in oak," David says, continuing the lesson as he pours you a glass of their *Rappahannock Red,* "you're trading in a little of the fruitiness for the complexity of the oak." That's why Hartwood ages this particular wine in stainless steel only. The blend of Chambourcin and three other varieties is typical of the Beaujolais style of reds—"unoaked, lighter, fruitier." It's a transitional which David likes to call their red wine with training wheels. Their Chardonnay, on the other hand, is aged in American oak barrels. It sports a very distinctive nose, with sturdy aromas of fruit that hold their own nicely against the influence of the oak.

The covered deck off the tasting room offers an elevated, close-up view of exactly one acre of Beverly's immaculately kept vines. The Livingstons, who live on the premises, often have supper here after the winery closes. While it's open, you can sit here and fine tune your aroma discernment skills as you unravel the complexities in a glass of *Rappahannock Red* or any of the other excellent wines to be sampled at this small winery.

While his wines can be intriguingly complex, Jim Livingston's summation of how an elementary school librarian came to be the owner of a winery is characteristically uncomplicated: "I just wanted to do it and I did it." With a little help from his friends.

Linden Vineyards

Linden Vineyards
3708 Harrels Corner Road
Linden, VA 22642

Hours: 11 a.m. to 5 p.m. Wednesday through Sunday from April through November. 11 a.m. to 5 p.m. Saturday and Sunday from December through March. Closed Easter Sunday, Thanksgiving, Christmas holidays, and New Year's Day.

Directions: From **I-66,** take exit 13 at Linden and go 1 mile east on Rte. 55. Turn right onto Rte. 638 and go 2 miles to winery, on the right. From **Rte. 211,** take Rte. 522 north to Rte. 55 east to Rte 638. Turn right onto Rte. 638 and go 2 miles to winery entrance, on the right. From **Richmond,** take I-95 north to **Fredericksburg,** then Rte. 17 north to business Rte. 29 north at **Warrenton.** Take Rte. 211 west and follow directions above.

Phone: 540-364-1997
Fax: 540-364-3894
E-mail: linden@crosslink.net
Website: www.lindenvineyards.com

Tasting fee: None

Wines: Vineyard designated Chardonnay and Sauvignon Blanc, red Bordeaux blends, ice wine

Picnic area? Yes

Owner: Jim Law
Winemaker: Jim Law

Perhaps it's because Jim Law's favorite place is outside in the vineyards that his winery seems designed as much to keep you outdoors as to draw you inside. The desire to linger in the open air starts in the parking lot, where a low fieldstone wall separates your vehicle from a rowdy patch of black-eyed Susans. Directly behind them slender, decorous rose bushes grace the starting posts of grapevine trellises converging towards the crest of the hill—creating in the visitor an urge to climb the hard, rocky slope along with the Cabernet Sauvignon.

In early April the cherry trees at the front of the winery are a major deterrent to anyone wishing to enter, and even if you can make it past them without stopping to drink in the fragrance of their pale pink blossoms, the benches at either end of the porch are a final enticement to remain outside just a little while longer.

Once you're inside and sampling Linden's wines, anticipation of moving onto the deck runs almost as high as enthusiasm for moving on to the next selection on the list. The retail area is on the ground level, but the chalet-style winery is built on an incline, so the wooden terrace off the tasting room puts you a story above. Here you'll find the pleasures you experience while sipping one of Jim's wines are enhanced by a panorama of green hills, rolling vineyards, and silver ponds.

In winter, a fire in the wood stove in the tasting room will keep your aft regions toasty while you appreciate the subtle beauties of vineyard dormancy from behind the thermal barrier of plate glass doors.

Jim loves working in the fields and in the cellar, but his management style in each is completely different. "We're very much control freaks in the vineyard," he says. "We do a lot of crop thinning because we like low yields—since they produce more intense wines. But once we get into the winery, we are super-minimums. We don't like to interfere with the wine at all." Jim doesn't do any fining, for example, to reduce bitterness. If a wine is out of balance, he prefers to just not use it. He also does as little filtering as possible.

Consequently most of Jim's time in the cellar is spent making blending decisions or performing basic winemaking tasks, like punching down his red wines by hand. He ferments his reds in one-ton bins. "Punching down is my favorite part," he confesses. "That's when you really get to know the wine. It develops different hot spots, and you have to keep mixing them up. In the center the wine could be ninety degrees and the outside could be sixty." The recipe has a familiar ring: simmer slowly, stirring occasionally.

There are seventeen acres of vinifera and hybrid grapes on the winery property. In addition, Jim buys fruit from several staff members who have become interested in grape growing while working at the winery and now have their own small vineyards in neighboring counties. Rather than always blending these grapes, Jim often celebrates the unique flavor and aroma qualities derived from the different soils and microclimates in which they're grown by producing vineyard-designated varietals that give credit to his employees' grape growing skills—skills they no doubt learned from him.

Jim first realized that he wanted to start a vineyard and winery while he was in the Peace Corps in Zaire, working with farmers there and instructing them in improved methods of growing fruit crops. Scratch this winemaker by choice and you'll find that, like most professionals who love what they do, Jim is a teacher by compulsion. Mention during a tasting that you feel a little uncertain about your ability to correctly identify the myriad flavors and aromas to be experienced in wines and he will pull out an organoleptic chart—"aroma wheel" in the vernacular—designed by enologists to assist the underconfident with aroma recall. If you notice out loud that the wheel doesn't tell you which aromas you're supposed to identify in which wines, Jim will admonish you in teacherly fashion that the idea is to assist you in developing a useful and enjoyable skill—not help you cheat at the bar with associations learned by rote.

Linden Vineyards is located between the fertile pasture lands of northern Virginia's horse country and the state's agricultural superstar, the Shenandoah Valley, on land that goes by the unvarnished description of hard scrabble. Farm abandonment, according to Jim, became epidemic here beginning in the 1920s. The thin-soiled, rocky, and hilly terrain seems to have discovered its agricultural niche in grape growing, however. Jim is happy that his vineyards are returning the land to productive farm use, while at the same time helping to stem the rising tide of development in Fauquier County.

This extremely popular winery produces about 5,000 cases a year of mostly dry wines, and Jim doesn't want to get much bigger than that. "If I did," he says, "I wouldn't be able to keep doing the things I really enjoy." Depending on the time of year, these would be micro-managing his wines in the vineyards or letting them explore their own options in the winery.

Loudoun Valley Vineyards

Loudoun Valley Vineyards
38516 Charlestown Pike
Waterford, VA 20197

Hours: 11 a.m. to 5 p.m. Friday, Saturday, and Sunday from April through December. 11 a.m. to 5 p.m. Saturday and Sunday from January through March.

Directions: From **D.C. and northern Virginia,** take Dulles Toll Road to Greenway to Leesburg. From **Leesburg,** take Rte. 7 west for 2 miles to Rte. 9 west and go 5 miles to winery, on the right.

Phone: 540-882-3375
E-mail: wine@loudounvalley-vineyards.com
Website: www.loudounvalley-vineyards.com

Tasting fee: None, except for groups of over 8 people

Wines: Cabernet Sauvignon, Merlot, Pinot Noir, Sangiovese, Nebbiolo, Chardonnay, Riesling, Sauvignon Blanc, Gamay, red Zinfandel, blush Zinfandel

Wine related items for sale? Yes
Picnic area? Yes
Food available? Light snacks
Facilities for private functions? Yes, for corporate gatherings only

Owners: Hubert and Dolores Tucker
Winemaker/Viticulturist: Hubert Tucker

What could wine grape vineyards in Virginia possibly have in common with the lunar landing module? Both tend to do well under fairly dry conditions on somewhat rugged terrain—and Hubert Tucker has had a hand in designing and launching both.

The owner and winemaker at Loudoun Valley Vineyards has spent much of his adult life in the aeronautics and space industry, including time working on the Apollo moon missions in Houston. He has always been interested in winegrowing and winemaking, and while employed at Cornell Labs in upstate New York, he purchased sixty acres in the Finger Lakes district and planted grapes, which he sold to the Taylor Wine Company.

In the late seventies a job change brought Hubert and his wife, Dolores, to the Washington area. They immediately began searching Maryland and Virginia for suitable vineyard sites. They soon found a twenty-six-acre parcel near the town of Waterford and in the early eighties began planting grapes. While they waited for the new vines to mature, the Tuckers started a nursery and grafting business. Today they are shipping grafted vinifera vines to twenty states, as well as selling to other Virginia vineyards.

Dolores and Hubert have four acres of rootstock—disease resistant native American vines that do not bear fruit but are grown just for the new wood they produce. Shoots, or canes, that have reached a certain diameter are harvested from the parent vines and spliced to cuttings—called scions—from European (vinifera) vines grown at Loudoun Valley. Modern grafting is done mechanically. The Tuckers have five German-made machines that make complementary incisions in the rootstock and the vinifera vine to create a union that resembles tongue-and-groove in woodworking. The graft section is then coated with wax and the composite vine is placed in a "callusing" room, where it stays for several weeks in a temperature-controlled environment while the graft hardens and the rootstock base forms its own plant roots. The vine is then field grown for a year, after which it can be dug up and shipped to other vineyards.

A few years after the Tuckers bought their property, more land became available next door. Soon after acquiring it, they planted additional grapes. Between the two adjoining tracts there are currently twenty-eight acres under vine at Loudoun Valley. There was a house under construction on the new parcel at the time Hubert and Dolores purchased it. They redesigned the structure, tearing out existing walls and making other changes to open up the interior and make it suitable as a winery. The tank room and barrel cellar occupy the lower level, and an overlook adjacent to the hospitality area upstairs offers visitors a visual synopsis of the production area below.

Loudoun Valley makes dry and semi-dry wines from traditional French, German, and Italian grapes. Their *Classic White,* however, is an off-dry blend of the very familiar

Riesling and several lesser known European varieties like Grüner Veltliner, Scheurebe, and French Colombard—providing what may be a new taste experience for even the most sophisticated and well-travelled palate. Depending on the vintage, they also offer Zinfandel in its unrestrained red varietal form, or as its much tamer alter ego—the ever popular blush, or white, Zinfandel.

In the tasting room there are lots of tables and chairs and plenty of time for enjoying a glass of wine from the cellar and a light lunch or snack of imported cheese, paté, and French bread from the pantry. The wraparound deck offers the same, plus a live view of vineyards and mountains—the Blue Ridge from one vantage point and the Catoctins from another.

Nearby Waterford was settled by Quakers in 1733 and grew up around a gristmill, established where it was because of the area's abundant supply of water. Annually, in October, the quaint little town receives over 30,000 visitors during a three-day home and craft show, one of the largest held anywhere in the country.

The fields in which the vineyards at Loudoun Valley were planted are rich in Civil War artifacts, like rifle bullets and Union belt buckles. Mosby's Rangers rode through here often, aided and abetted by farmers who supplied provisions for the men and their horses. At one point a frustrated Union army sent a force of 4,000 men, who were camped on the property for several months, to try to capture the nettlesome Confederate colonel and his band of raiders. Of course they never did. Given the Gray Ghost's extraordinary talent for remaining at large, they may as well have sent a mission to look for him on the moon.

Naked Mountain Vineyard

Naked Mountain Vineyard
2747 Leeds Manor Road
Markham, VA 22643

Hours: 11 a.m. to 5 p.m. Wednesday through Sunday and selected Monday holidays from March through December; weekends only during January and February. Closed Thanksgiving, Christmas, and New Year's Day.

Directions: From **D.C.,** take I-66 west to exit 18 (Markham). Take Rte. 688 north for 1.5 miles to winery. From **Richmond,** take I-95 north to **Fredericksburg.** Take Rte. 17 north. Follow signs for Rte. 17 to I-66. Take I-66 west to exit 18 (Markham). Take Rte. 688 north for 1.5 miles to the winery entrance.

Phone: 540-364-1609
Fax: 540-364-4870
Website: www.nakedmtn.com

Tasting fee: None, except $3 per person for groups of 10 or more. Groups over 10, please call for appointment.

Wines: Chardonnay, Riesling, Sauvignon Blanc, Cabernet Sauvignon, Cabernet Franc

Wine related items for sale? Yes
Picnic area? Yes
Food available? Light snacks

Owners: Robert and Phoebe Harper
Winemaker: Joe B. Sullivan III

It's possible, even probable, that Naked Mountain was given its intriguing moniker by none other than George Washington, who was the first person to survey the land in this part of northern Virginia. According to Bob Harper, the name goes back at least as far as 1765 when it appeared as "*the* naked mountain" on the first deed to property owned by the family of John Marshall, the nation's fourth chief justice.

Bob and his wife, Phoebe, acquired their forty-two-acre parcel on the mountain in 1973, and in 1976 they planted a quarter-acre vineyard with the intention of making hobbyist wine for themselves. By 1980 the all-vinifera vineyard had grown to five acres and Bob's winemaking skills had matured to the point that he decided to leave a sales career with an international oil company and turn his part-time avocation into a full-time profession.

An addition to the original winery, which opened in 1981, is now the fermentation and barrel-aging facility for Naked Mountain's widely acclaimed Chardonnay, which accounts for over half the wine Bob produces. Rather than destemming and crushing these grapes, Bob whole-cluster presses them to minimize the time between the moment the skins are broken and the juice is safely in the tank—where it won't spoil and won't oxidize. This method also reduces the nonsoluble solids in the juice, as well as the bitter phenols. Bob uses only French oak for barrel-fermenting and aging his Chardonnay because it contains more of the flavonoid phenol vanillin—the chief flavor component in vanilla—than American oak does. Farther up the mountainside a chalet-style building constructed in 1984 houses the tasting room, the winery where Bob vints his other wines, and another barrel cellar.

Naked Mountain now has eight acres of vines at the winery site and leases additional acreage at two nearby vineyards. The Harpers still grow only vinifera grapes, and most of their wines are fermented dry. Even the residual sugar in their Riesling is usually in the modest 2 to 3 percent range.

In 1997, however, nature provided a rare opportunity which Bob could not pass up. Botrytis, or "bunch rot," is a disease that attacks grapes, causing them to rot on the vine. But if it appears late in the ripening cycle, this normally devastating fungus can produce a beneficial condition in varieties such as Chardonnay, Sauvignon Blanc, and Riesling which German winegrowers call "the noble rot." As Bob explains it, "The fungus lives on the skin of the grape, leeching out the water and concentrating everything else—the sugar, acid, and flavors of the fruit. It also lends a honey-like flavor of its own." The organism requires cool weather to grow, something seldom encountered in Virginia close to harvest. "But in 1997," Bob recalls, "we had an unusually cool August and September, and a good deal of the noble rot developed on our Riesling. As a result we made a dessert wine out of this variety. Some individual berries," he notes, "had sugar weights as high as 45 percent." Bunch rot, it seems, has both a good side and a bad side.

Not so the downy mildew. In the nineteenth century, this disease native to America nearly destroyed the winemaking industry in France. A prevention was discovered in the "Bordeaux mixture," but the cure was almost as bad as the disease. The spray, consisting of copper sulfate and lime, had the unhealthy side effect of burning the leaves. Roses were observed to be even more susceptible to downy mildew than grapes, so winegrowers began planting the harbinger flowers amid their vines. If the disease showed itself on the leaves of the rosebushes, then, and only then, were the vines subjected to their harsh medicine. Today, gentler treatments keep wine grapes free of the mildew, and the roses serve mainly as traditional embellishments to vineyards like Bob and Phoebe's.

The natural corks used at Naked Mountain come from Sicily, where the people making them may not know that the winery's slogan imprinted on its bottle stoppers encourages customers to "Drink Naked." The invitation refers to Bob's wines, of course. In the tasting room, standard winery-hopping attire is required. Should you leave your wrap in the car, however, the fire that Bob and Phoebe keep going in the tasting room on winter weekends will keep you warm enough while you enjoy a glass of their wine and a plate of homemade sausage or vegetable lasagna made fresh by a local chef. The stones for the twenty-two-foot-wide fireplace surround came out of Bob's fields. Stone houses and stone fences are everywhere in the little towns and along the country roads of northern Virginia, and you wouldn't expect to find a stone left unturned. But according to Bob, "they grow," and there's a new crop every spring.

You'll find a few coming up down by the pond, where the mood in summer is—oh—*naturel*. Unselfconscious, foot-long koi glide up in the altogether and look you in the eye, while out in the middle of the water, something shimmering streaks into the air to catch a flying snack. It's cool at the picnic tables under the trees. Or spread your lunch on a blanket and expect to be here a while. The invitation is irresistible: Relax. Watch the fish jump and the rocks grow.

Oasis Winery

> Oasis Winery
> 14141 Hume Road
> Hume, VA 22639
>
> **Hours:** Open daily year round. Tastings: 10 a.m. to 5 p.m. Tours at 1 p.m. and 3 p.m. Closed Thanksgiving, Christmas, and New Year's Day.
>
> **Directions:** From **D.C.,** take I-66 west to exit 27 (Marshall). Take a left after exiting then an immediate right onto Rte. 647. Go 4 miles and turn right onto Rte. 635. Go 10 miles to the winery, on the left. From **Skyline Drive or Front Royal,** take Rte. 522 south for 7 miles and turn left onto Rte. 635. Go 1 mile to winery, on the right. From **Richmond** via Warrenton, take I-95 north to Rte. 17 north into Warrenton. Take Rte. 211 west for 18 miles, then Rte. 522 north for 8 miles, then right on Rte. 635 for 1 mile.
>
> **Phone:** 800-304-7656 or 540-635-7627
> **Fax:** 540-635-GOLD
> **E-mail:** oasiswine@aol.com
> **Website:** www.oasiswine.com
> **AOL keyword:** Oasis Wine
>
> **Tasting fee:** $3 per person (Includes souvenir wine glass.)
>
> **Wines:** Cabernet Sauvignon, Merlot, Chardonnay, Riesling, Gewürztraminer, *Meritage,* Oasis *Brut* sparkling wine
>
> **Wine related items for sale?** Yes
> **Picnic area?** Yes
> **Food available?** Casual gourmet fare: light snacks, light restaurant fare
> **Special Programs?** Club Oasis
> **Facilities for private functions?** Yes
>
> **Owner:** Oasis Vineyards, Inc.
> **Winemaker/Viticulturist:** Tareq Salahi

At the northern gateway to the Skyline Drive is a distinctively shaped mountain, an ancient geologic upheaval softened by aging to a smooth-edged pyramid. As you make your way along winding Route 635, it constantly shifts its position in your line of sight, eventually coming to a standstill behind the gates of Oasis Winery. On the eastern side of the Peak, as the mountain is called, the oldest Cabernet Sauvignon and Merlot vines in the state are thriving. From vintage to vintage they validate the decision of Dirgham Salahi to plant traditional European grapes where they were once believed impossible to grow, namely, anywhere in Virginia.

From the beginning this winery has done things differently. In 1979 Dirgham brought in custom fermentation tanks from Italy. Made of concrete, they had to be set in place by crane and the winery built around them. You won't find their likes on any other tour in Virginia. Emblazoned in high relief with the grape-cluster emblem of the manufacturer and the Oasis insignia, they stand in two immovable rows at the bottom of the stairway leading from the tasting room to the cellar.

Tareq Salahi is CEO at Oasis, and he remembers helping parents Dirgham and Corinne plant the original vines when he was only seven years old. The initial 15 acres have grown to just over 100. To the original varieties, which also included a block of Chardonnay, they've added Cabernet Franc, Pinot Noir, Riesling, and Gewürztraminer—and for blending purposes, an acre of Viognier. The vines are closely spaced, 1,000 per acre. "We employ the traditional Bordeaux dense planting," says Tareq. "This lowers the yield, which increases the fruit intensity and character intensity of the grapes, enabling us to create very complex wines." The harvest is between 2 and 2½ tons per acre, from which Oasis produces about 20,000 cases a year. This tight spacing of vines has paid off in a room full of trophies and medals.

In 1997, Oasis received an accolade which had never been accorded an American label before. That year *Wine Enthusiast* magazine placed the Virginia winery's *Brut* on its list of the top ten sparkling wines in the world—shoulder to shoulder with champagne luminaries Krug, Moët's *Dom Pérignon,* et al. The Oasis *Brut* is so good, in fact, it's served at the French Embassy in Washington as a welcoming toast to visiting dignitaries. Out of respect for the region of France where the most elegant of wines was invented, Oasis uses only the terms *sparkling wine, bubbly,* or other champagne synonyms when speaking about their own wines.

Sparkling wine is normally about one-third of production at Oasis, but that can vary, Tareq says, "depending on what Mother Nature does to us in the vineyard. Not every year do we make our sparkling wine. It must be an exquisite year." When they are producing, the recipe is always the same: a *cuvée* of 60 percent Chardonnay and 40 percent Pinot Noir. *Cuvée* refers to an elegant blend and is a term traditionally reserved for champagne making, although, as Tareq points out, it can also be used appropriately when blending still wines "to create something very beautiful or very special."

Oasis uses *méthode champenoise,* the identical technique used in the Champagne region of France. After the finished wines are blended and bottled, sugar and yeast are added to the still wine, and the bottle is sealed with a pry-up cap. Fermentation in the bottle takes about ninety days. The Oasis *Brut* is then aged for a minimum of five years and their *Brut Cuvée D'Or* for a minimum of eight. The tiny bubbles produced in the *Brut* and even tinier ones in the *Cuvée D'Or* are in direct proportion to the time each spends in undisturbed repose.

After their extended beauty rest, the wines are gently nudged awake by the process of riddling. The bottles are placed in a rack with necks pointing down and each day for approximately two months given a quarter turn to the right, by hand. This slowly moves the lees created during the second fermentation toward the neck. When the collection of by-product is complete, the bottle necks are quick-frozen in a sub-zero solution of water and glycol so that during disgorgement the sediment will be expelled, in a quasi-orderly fashion, into a waiting receptacle. If you're touring the winery while this is going on, you'll hear the loud pops when the caps come off and the frozen bullets shoot out. It's at this point that the *dosage* is administered. Unlike the *cuvée,* the *dosage* is a closely guarded secret for every champagne house. "To give you an idea of what it could be," Tareq says, "it could be wine or juice from the winery. It could be an Armagnac or Cognac, raspberry or strawberry liqueur, or a combination of all these things." At Oasis it hasn't changed since they put up their first bottle of sparkling wine in 1980.

After napping for up to eight years, a day that includes disgorgement, *dosage,* corking, and caging can be exhausting for even the most effervescent of wines. At Oasis their bubbly is allowed to recuperate for twenty-four hours before the bottles are hand-washed, foiled, labeled, and packaged.

Meritage is an American coinage that signifies a marrying of three Bordeaux reds: Cabernet Sauvignon, Cabernet Franc, and Merlot. At Oasis these finished wines are bottled together in equal proportions. The result is a blend with the bigness and boldness of Cabernet Sauvignon, softened by the tannic temperance of the Merlot and Cabernet Franc. This winning combination earned Oasis a double gold medal at the Taster's Guild International Competition. After being

Oasis Winery

given a perfect score by all of the judges, the wine was submitted to each of them again at a later date. Unaware they were judging a previously tasted wine, all ten gave the Oasis Meritage another perfect score.

Enjoying it with food is an integral part of today's wine experience. At Oasis they would add another dimension—entertainment—and here the emphasis is on action verbs. From June through September the winery hosts a weekly event called Polo, Wine, and Twilight Dine. At Great Meadow near the Plains, Virginia, or at Potomac Polo Club in Maryland, you can enjoy a catered meal and a bottle of wine in safety and comfort while Tareq leads the champion Oasis team in this lightning-paced equine sport. His skill at the game has taken him to England and a match with Prince Charles at the Tidworth Polo Club. Following the event, Tareq was presented with a gold-hilt Millennium Sabre crafted by Firmin and Sons, who were appointed by the queen to fabricate the commemorative swords.

On the occasional Saturday afternoon at the winery, Tareq uses his saber to practice the centuries-old custom of *sabrage*. This was once the preferred method of Europe's royalty for getting at the contents of a bottle of champagne, and Napoleon allegedly would not drink any that had not been opened this way. The barbarians, unwilling to cope with the intricacies of wire cage and cork, are said to have favored it as well. With the same swift precision with which he wields a polo mallet, Tareq makes short work of the neck of a bottle of brut.

If you come to the winery in August you can take part in another Oasis tradition, the annual Blessing of the Vines. The public is invited to join clergy and students from Christendom College, along with members of the international order of Knights of the Vine, in a preharvest procession through the vineyards. Gregorian chants and the Cross of the Millennium, designed by local sculptor Frederick Hart for Pope John Paul II's first visit to the U.S., set the tone for this ceremony of thanksgiving. Both *sabrage* and ritual processionals are showing up at other vineyards around the country, but it was Oasis that introduced these European customs into North American winemaking culture.

The spacious tasting room with floor-to-ceiling fieldstone fireplace is a comfortable spot at any time of year to enjoy a glass of wine and soak up some winery ambience. Outside at Oasis you're invited to unfold your tent, figuratively speaking, on the patio or the triple-tiered deck and take in the seasonal beauties of vineyards stretching out in all directions.

In terms of production, virtually every available acre at the current site is already under vines, and right now Oasis is happy where they are. Of winegrowing in Virginia, Tareq notes that the state will never get to the same level of production as California, for example, because it simply doesn't have the acreage to plant. While a lot more can be planted, the Virginia wine industry, he predicts, will always be one that focuses on premium wines. That is certainly the emphasis at this winery, where visitors will discover a marvelous *cuvée* of flamboyant custom and sacred tradition, spectacular scenery and Oasis *Brut*—the champagne of American sparkling wines.

89

Piedmont Vineyards & Winery

Piedmont Vineyards & Winery
2546D Halfway Road
Middleburg, VA 20117

Hours: 10 a.m. to 6 p.m. daily from April through December; 11 a.m. to 5 p.m. Wednesday through Sunday from January through March. Closed New Year's Day, Thanksgiving, and December 24, 25, and 31.

Directions: From **Middleburg**, go 3 miles south on Rte. 626. Winery is on the right. From **D.C.**, take I-66 to exit 31 at The Plains. Take a right at the exit, a right onto Rte. 55, and an immediate left onto Rte. 626. Go 5 miles to the winery, on the left.

Phone: 540-687-5528
Fax: 540-687-5777
E-mail: info@piedmontwines.com
Website: www.piedmontwines.com

Tasting fee: $3 per person, applied to wine purchase

Wines: *Native Yeast Chardonnay, Special Reserve Chardonnay, Hunt Country Chardonnay,* Sémillon, Cabernet Sauvignon

Wine related items for sale? Yes
Picnic area? Yes
Food available? Light snacks
Facilities for private functions? Yes

Owners: Gerhard von Finck, Frank Löwentraut, Hans Fabian
Winemaker/Viticulturist: John Fitter

Located at the epicenter of Virginia horse country, the fields surrounding Piedmont Vineyards have experienced many a flying divot as fox hunters pounded across its terroir in pursuit of the cunning canine, which in this part of the commonwealth numbers almost as many as the horses themselves. It was her love of the favorite pastime of the English—and northern Virginia—leisure class that brought the founder of this winery all the way from Chicago to Middleburg. On one of her many fox hunts during the 1930s and 1940s Elizabeth Furness caught sight of Piedmont and its then neglected Greek Revival house. In 1943 she persuaded her husband to buy the 500-acre dairy farm, with the intention of reviving that operation. By 1971 Elizabeth could see that dairying was not going to be profitable and decided to plant grapes instead. Never one to shrink from a challenge, she chose Chardonnay. In 1973 Piedmont became the first vineyard in Virginia in modern times to plant and successfully grow this vinifera variety.

Piedmont's raison d'être is—and always has been—Chardonnay. They are currently producing three styles of America's most popular white varietal. Their *Native Yeast Chardonnay* is fermented with wild yeast. Piedmont was the first Virginia winery to use native yeast in the production of wine. Winemaker John Fitter goes out about a week before harvest and picks fruit off one or two rows, presses the grapes, and fills several five-gallon glass carboys about two-thirds full with the juice. In about a week the spontaneously fermented wine is used to inoculate the rest of the lot. All three of Piedmont's Chardonnays go through malolactic fermentation, and again the winemaker has chosen the natural method. ML bacteria are abundant at the winery—in the barrels, the air, the walls—and John never has to augment the process by inoculation with a nonresident strain.

The winemaker here is committed to intervening as little as possible in the natural winemaking process, preferring to carefully guide and monitor rather than manipulate. The only

wine he filters is the *Hunt Country Chardonnay* and then only because it contains ½ percent residual sugar. "I can't put wine in a bottle with sugar in it," he explains, "without making sure it's not going to ferment again." As for the other wines, they sit in their barrels and settle out. "We may rack them a couple of times," John says, "to move the wines off the solids, and generally they fall out clear. Knowing that it tastes good and has nice aromas is more important. I don't care if the wine isn't sparklingly clear. If it's clear, that's good enough for me." It's apparently good enough for the *Wine Spectator* too. John proudly recalls when the prestigious publication gave Piedmont's '93 *Special Reserve Chardonnay* a 91-point score, the highest they'd given any American wine that wasn't produced on the West Coast.

They are vinifera purists at Piedmont, growing, besides Chardonnay, a little Cabernet Sauvignon and Cabernet Franc. They're also one of the few Virginia vineyards growing Sémillon—a cautious five acres. This Bordeaux variety is somewhat persnickety. "It's always either too hot or too cold," says office manager Linda Ridgeway, "and the crop is usually very sparse." John explains that Sémillon is very thin-skinned and extremely susceptible to rot. Until 1999 Piedmont had not been able to produce any since 1993. That vintage won four gold medals and seven silver the very next year. Apparently Virginia-grown Sémillon is like the girl with the curl in the middle of her forehead: when it's good, it's very, very good, but when it's bad, it's—well, not the stuff wine is made of, and John simply has to dump the juice and hope that next year will be better.

The winery at Piedmont is in the dairy barn; the office is in the milk house; and a former connecting breezeway now houses the tasting room. The original dirt floor has been paved with flagstones. Glass doors lead to a small tree-canopied deck at the entrance. On a busy Saturday or Sunday, the constant sliding and bumping of the doors reminds the owners that the charmingly decorated hospitality room really is too small. The horse barn, just across the crush pad from the winery, has been tapped as the prospective new tasting room. Visitors might even suggest that the corncrib in the field across from the parking lot would make an excellent pavilion. There are picnic tables in the meadow next to the spring house. Combination stone and split-rail fences, the preferred form of property delineation in northern Virginia, enclose the meadow and the vineyards and line the driveway past the house to the winery.

The mansion has grown from a one-room structure that dates back to the 1730s and is not surprisingly a Virginia Historic Landmark. Completely restored by the Furnesses in the forties, it is available today as a venue for corporate meetings and wedding receptions.

Piedmont's current ninety-five acres—twenty-six in vines—are nestled among some very large estates. On the winery side of the road there are only two other farms between the vineyards and the town of Middleburg three miles away. In keeping with the reserve of the neighborhood and the stately elegance of the house, things at Piedmont are quiet and low key. Except for an occasional wine and food pairing, activities consist entirely of growing wine, making wine, and selling wine. And awfully good wine at that.

Shadwell-Windham Winery

Shadwell-Windham Winery
14727 Mountain Road
Hillsboro, VA 20132

Hours: Noon to 6 p.m. on Saturdays and 2 p.m. to 6 p.m. on Sundays from March through December. Closed January and February and on Easter, Thanksgiving, and Christmas. Beginning March 2001, check website for new hours.

Directions: From **D.C.**, take I-66 west to Rte. 267. Continue on to Leesburg and take Rte. 7 west to Rte. 9 west towards Hillsboro. Go 7.3 miles and turn right onto Mountain Road (Rte. 690 north). Winery is 1 mile on the left.

Phone: 540-668-6464
Fax: 540-668-9052
Website:
www.shadwellwindham.com

Tasting fee: None

Wines: Chardonnay, Riesling, Sauvignon Blanc, Viognier, Merlot, Cabernet Sauvignon, Cabernet Franc

Picnic area? Yes
Facilities for private functions? Yes

Owners: George and Nicki Bazaco
Winemakers/Viticulturists: the Bazacos

Shadwell-Windham is a small and thoroughly inviting Virginia winery in the process of becoming a larger and even more inviting one. The owners of Windham estate near Hillsboro are currently producing about 700 cases of wine a year. Their stated goal is 2,000 cases by the year 2002. To accommodate the increase in volume, they need larger facilities.

For the first five years, winemaking here involved some rather intensive logistics. The grapes were crushed and pressed on a concrete slab outside the horse barn. Barrel fermentation, aging, and bottling, however, took place some distance from the barn in the basement of Windham's rambling, antebellum farmhouse. Customers wanting to taste George and Nicki Bazaco's wines descended wooden steps into the cellar through an outside hatchway. Sampling of the wines was done at a plain folding table in the subterranean tasting room in intimate proximity to French and American oak barrels and paraphernalia of small-winery genre.

The new facilities at this farm winery are taking shape where the red barn used to be. The old structure was dismantled in the fall of 1999, right after crush. The production area, which was completed in time for the harvest of 2000, will have a new barn built around it. The tanks and the barrels are down in the basement, as they were when the wine was being sold from the house. The tasting room, which is scheduled to be finished in 2001, will be on the ground floor and will serve double duty as the library. In this case the Bazacos are referring not to wine but to books. George practices pulmonary critical-care medicine in the Greater Washington area, and he and Nicki will eventually move to the farm and live in an apartment above the winery.

Customers will taste the same kinds of wines at the new facility that they enjoyed in the old cellar. Shadwell-Windham grows only vinifera grapes and makes all dry wines. The only hint of sweetness you'll normally find in their vintages is the ½ percent of residual sugar in the Alsatian-style Riesling. George and Nicki's list includes three Bordeaux varietals—Cabernet Sauvignon, Cabernet Franc, and Merlot—as well as two styles of Chardonnay and a blended white from Sauvignon Blanc and Viognier.

The deck and patio of the new tasting room will provide comfortable spots for sipping wine and watching the shadows drift on Short Hill Mountain not far away at the edge of the farm. Or you can focus your attention on activities in the weeping–willow-lined pond even closer to where you're sitting. Periodically a resident gaggle of geese will line up single file and make a stately, if somewhat noisy, procession across the water, only to queue up again shortly thereafter and head back, their mysterious mission apparently accomplished—or perhaps not.

Dr. Bazaco hints that the silo next to the old barn site has the potential of becoming an observatory at some point down the road. In the meantime it makes an interesting subject for art groups that regularly come to the farm to sketch its landscape and its buildings. No one knows for certain what the shed behind the house was for, but its fieldstone construction and the intriguing vertical slit windows in the eighteen-inch-thick walls make it one of the artists' favorite subjects.

George's mother, Hope Bazaco, is a second-generation Greek-American grandmother with incredible energy and typical Aegean warmth and openness. Cooking is a favorite pastime, and in the same way that farmers' wives in Greece and in this country used to prepare meals for the hired help, she fixes lunch or dinner for all the hands that show up to volunteer during harvest and crush. Her grandfather had a vineyard on the outskirts of Kirklerali, a small town in northern Greece, and her grandmother made and sold wine vinegar to earn a little money for herself. Hope, who lives on the farm, makes red wine vinegar for friends and family, too. The New York girl who grew up in the Bronx also has a garden outside the former tasting room and puts up her own fruits and vegetables every summer.

Hope has compiled a book of precepts taught her by her mother, who immigrated to America alone at the age of only fifteen. The slender volume is for sale at the winery and offers familiar admonitions that most of us would do well to heed. Virginia's winegrowers already know the importance of the three *D*s: dedication, determination, and discipline. "Procrastination is the thief of time" is a Dickensian call to those who have been thinking about it and talking about it to get up off their good intentions, get out, and discover for themselves the abundance of fine wines being made at Virginia farm wineries like Shadwell-Windham.

Spotted Tavern Winery

Spotted Tavern Winery and Dodd's Cider Mill
Dodd's Corner
Route 612
Hartwood, VA 22471

Hours: Noon to 4 p.m. Saturday and Sunday from April through December. Closed January through March, with tours available by appointment only. Closed Thanksgiving and Christmas.

Directions: From the intersection of I-95 and Rte. 17 at **Fredericksburg,** go north on Rte. 17 for 5 miles. Turn right onto Rte. 612 (Hartwood Road) and go 4 miles to white stucco building on the left. From **Richmond,** take I-95 north to Fredericksburg and follow the directions above. From **D.C.,** take I-95 south to Rte. 17 north at Fredericksburg and follow directions above. From the **Charlottesville** area, take Rte. 29 north to Rte. 17 south. Turn left onto Rte. 612 (Hartwood Road) and go 4 miles to white stucco building on the left.

Phone: 540-752-4453
Fax: 540-752-4611
Tasting fee: None

Wines: *MoonBeam Hard Cider,* sparkling cider, fresh cider in season, *Stonehouse White*

Wine related items for sale? Yes, seasonal

Owners: John and Cathy Harris
Winemaker/Viticulturist: John Harris

This is the only winery in Virginia today that was making a vinted product prior to Prohibition. In 1912, Robert E. Lee Dodd, who operated several mills at Dodd's Corner near Fredericksburg, purchased a cider press on credit and began producing hard cider. Over four decades after Reconstruction, times were still hard in this part of Virginia, and cash was the shortest commodity in supply. Customers would bring their own apples to Dodd's Mill to be ground and pressed. The mill would hold back a portion of the juice as payment in kind. It then fermented that juice to make hard cider. Part of the mill workers' wages was a per diem of a gallon of cider, wisely paid in installments throughout the day. This method of compensation served the establishment well during the Depression, too.

The mill even managed to stay open after the production of alcoholic beverages came under statewide ban in 1914, several years ahead of the rest of the country. Dodd's continued to grind and press apples into fresh cider. Some customers no doubt took it home and made what was known as farmhouse cider. The fresh juice, laden with the native yeast that was on the apples when they were picked, was pumped into a barrel, the barrel hole was bunged, and a slow, natural, cool-temperature fermentation occurred over the winter. In the spring those Stafford County residents had hard cider. In this manner they were able to circum-*vint* a law predestined for revocation, and Dodd's Mill did its part, however unwittingly, to mitigate the inconvenience of Prohibition.

In 1982 a fire at the complex destroyed the sawmill, the planing mill, and the flour mill—everything except the cider press—and Dodd's virtually closed down until 1995. These days John Harris and wife Cathy, who is Dodd's great-granddaughter, are using the original turn-of-the-century press to make a cider that John modestly describes as "the elixir of the gods, the temptation of Eve, Nirvana in a bottle." *MoonBeam* hard cider is made in the Brittany manner using a strain of champagne yeast instead of native yeast, and the process is similar to that of making sparkling wine. This French-style cider is sweeter, fruitier, and has slightly less carbonation than the harder, more completely fermented English version. The English find it entirely to their liking, however. A motorcade bearing a member of an official British delegation once showed up unexpectedly at the mill. The cider was tasted and several cases ordered for a party at the embassy in Washington that evening. A word of caution: Just because it's put up in similar style bottles and kegs, do not think that *MoonBeam* has the same alcohol content as beer. Whereas the latter contains 3½ to 4 percent, this hard cider registers anywhere from 6.0 to 8.0 on the potency scale.

In addition to *MoonBeam,* which is classified as a fruit wine by the licensing authorities, the Harrises also produce wine from grapes. Spotted Tavern Winery's *Stonehouse White,* the only traditional wine they make, is an award-winning blend of Seyval, Riesling, and Vidal.

Dodd's also produces a sparkling cider. Not to be confused with hard cider—which also sparkles—this beverage is made from the same proprietary blend of seven kinds of apples used to make their *MoonBeam.* The juice, however, is pasteurized to prevent fermentation. Instead, carbon dioxide is added to give this nonalcoholic cider its effervescence.

And in case you're yearning for the experience of making your own hard cider, Dodd's Mill produces fresh, unpasteurized cider in season, which you may take to your own farm, home in the suburbs, or cidery in the city. A plastic gallon of Dodd's (with cap slightly unscrewed) placed in a quiet spot at the back of the refrigerator will, in about two weeks' time, yield an equal volume of delicious, refreshing farmhouse cider.

The cider mill and winery occupy a plain, stuccoed, block and concrete building, the only part of the establishment to survive the fire in 1982. But what Spotted Tavern may lack in looks it makes up for in personality. The winery side of the operation is named after an eighteenth-century ordinary that used to be located on the Harrises' farm. If he's there when you are, John will be happy to entertain you with the story of how the tavern got its spots. If you ask, he'll also oblige with an explanation of the difference between vinted products, like wine and cider, and brewed and distilled beverages, like beer and bourbon. His presentation is so lively, in fact, you'll think the term *regale* was invented here.

If you arrive during apple harvest, from September up until Christmas, you may get to see the cider press in operation. It's hard to miss. It occupies the entire front of the building, and you have to squeeze past it to get to the tasting room and retail sales area. Here you'll enjoy what for many will be a brand new and exceedingly delightful experience—Virginia hard cider made the way the Bretons like it.

Tart, crisp, juicy Winesaps, like these at Crown Orchard in Albemarle County, are the makings of delicious, refreshing Virginia hard cider.

Swedenburg Estate Vineyard

Swedenburg Estate Vineyard
23595 Winery Lane
Middleburg, VA 20117

Hours: 10 a.m. to 4 p.m. daily. Closed July 4th, Thanksgiving and Christmas.

Directions: From **D.C.**, take I-66 to Rte. 50 west and go 21 miles to the winery entrance, on the left. From **Middleburg**, go 1 mile east on Rte. 50 to the winery entrance, on the right. From **Richmond**, take I-95 north to **Fredericksburg.** Take Rte. 17 north to Rte. 245 at Great Meadow (right turn). Take Rte. 245 to Rte. 55 at the Plains. Turn right onto Rte. 55, go 1 block, then turn left onto Rte. 626 towards Middleburg. At Middleburg, turn right onto Rte. 50 and go 1 mile east to the winery, on the right. From the **Charlottesville** area, take Rte. 29 north to Rte. 17 north and follow the directions for Fredericksburg.

Phone: 540-687-5219

Tasting fee: $1 per person

Wines: Chardonnay, Riesling, Seyval Blanc, Pinot Noir, Cabernet Sauvignon

Facilities for private functions? Yes

Owners: W. A. Swedenburg family
Winemaker/Viticulturist: Juanita Swedenburg

Wayne Swedenburg had passed the farm on John Mosby Highway many times and cast admiring glances in its direction, wondering who owned such a beautiful piece of land with its broad fields sweeping gently towards the mountains. Wayne and his wife Juanita met while they were on assignment with the Foreign Service in Indochina. Both had grown up on farms in the Midwest and knew that they eventually wanted to settle down in a rural setting. When Wayne returned from a tour of duty in Laos in the late 1960s, Juanita, who had been farm hunting while he was away, took him out to see a property she had located on Route 50, less than a mile from the town of Middleburg. When they pulled up to the gate, Wayne recognized it immediately. "We don't need to go any further," he told her. "Just buy it!"

The 130 acres that now make up historic Valley View Farm were once part of Lord Fairfax's vast holdings in northern Virginia. A house was erected on the property in 1762, as required in the tenant lease executed by his lordship's nephew Bryan Fairfax. The sixteen-by-twenty-foot structure, with original fireplace, is now the dining room of the Swedenburgs' house. Most of the additions that have been made to the stone dwelling predate the Civil War.

The Swedenburgs started out growing timothy and clover, for which there was a ready market here in the heart of Virginia horse country. Now the tawny rolled bales of hay that dot their fields in spring and summer are for the purebred registered black Angus they raise. Most of the farm's open acreage is devoted to cattle. Fifteen acres of mostly vinifera grapes support the winemaking division of this family farm enterprise, which produces about 3,000 cases of wine per year.

For a number of years, while Wayne was still in the Service, the job of running the farm fell almost entirely on Juanita's shoulders. Even today if you're outside and happen to see a woman come racing across the fields toward the winery in an open farm-mobile, that will be Juanita. She is the winemaker at Swedenburg Estate Vineyard and has final say about what to grow and how it will be vinted. She also oversees the vineyards and has responsibility for the tasting room.

Wayne modestly describes his role in the operation as that of "cellar rat." His duties include crushing and pressing of the grapes at harvest, racking of the wines, and barrel maintenance. He also fills in for Juanita behind the bar, where he talks knowingly, and glowingly, about his wife's wines. The Swedenburgs will tell you quite candidly that they would rather be out of a particular wine, as they occasionally are, than release a vintage before they feel it is ready. Juanita's Cabernet Sauvignon usually spends two years in the barrel and another in the bottle. Their barrel-fermented Chardonnay will spend about seven months in lightly toasted French oak and get up to fifteen months of bottle aging. It's a Burgundy style white wine. "In other words," Wayne explains, "all of the components have melded together nicely and you don't really pick up much of the oak."

The winery also produces a French Alsatian-style Riesling, meaning an off-dry with less residual sugar (only 1 percent) than the typical German version (2 to 3 percent). Their Seyval is made in the French Chablis style: it is fermented in stainless steel at a very cold temperature to retain all of the fruitiness of the grape and never sees the inside of a barrel. The result is a smorgasbord of flavors and aromas from papaya to mango, spicy pear, almond, and citrus. They also make a Vidal Blanc, which is private-labeled under the Great Falls Vineyard label, so it's not available at the winery. However, you can order it with dinner at L'Auberge Chez Francois, a five-star restaurant located in Great Falls.

When it comes to grapes, the Swedenburgs firmly believe that Mother Nature knows best and don't do any irrigation or fertilization in the vineyards. Wayne points out that the soil in this area is limestone based, the same type of terroir that you find in Burgundy and Bordeaux, and is said to be very good for wine grapes and for horses. That may explain why there are so many vineyards and so many horses in this part of Virginia. On the odd Saturday morning a whole cluster of the latter, with eager riders astride, will assemble at Valley View Farm. As Wayne discovered when they bought the place, the previous owner was master of the Orange County Hunt, which originated in New York and is the oldest and most recognized hunt club in the U.S.

The winery, built in 1987, was designed with the primary stipulation that it not look like a commercial structure. With its stucco facade painted a soft earth tone, its modified quoins, and standing-seam tin roof, it looks more like a compact but exquisitely charming starter house. Hanging over the porch at the entrance is a wooden horse that bids you welcome in Swedish. The Dahla horse, named for the village in Sweden where it originated, is found in homes throughout Scandinavia. Inside, the tasting room is warm and inviting, with oriental rugs covering hardwood flooring. A richly colored tapestry, a handmade reproduction of a famous work that hangs in the Musée de Cluny in Paris, shows you what coopering and winemaking were like in the Middle Ages.

Just off the tasting room, there's a catwalk where you can get a full view of Wayne's super-orderly cellar.

As you leave the winery, the Dahla horse asks you to *komigen,* which really is Swedish for "come again." You'll surely want to take the Swedenburgs up on their invitation.

Tarara Vineyard & Winery

Tarara Vineyard and Winery
13648 Tarara Lane
Leesburg, VA 20176

Hours: 11 a.m. to 5 p.m. daily except Tuesday from March through December; weekends only during January and February.

Directions: From **Leesburg,** take Rte. 15 north approximately 8 miles to Lucketts. Turn right onto Rte. 662 and go 3 miles to the winery, on the left. From **Frederick, MD,** take Rte. 15 south. After crossing the Potomac River, go 2 miles and turn left onto Rte. 658. Go 2 miles, turn left onto Rte. 662, and go 1 mile to winery entrance, on the left.

Phone: 703-771-7100
703-478-8168 (Metro D.C.)
Website: www.tarara.com

Tasting fee: $2 per person

Wines: Cabernet Sauvignon, Cabernet Franc, Merlot, Chardonnay, Pinot Gris, *Terra Rouge, Wild River Red*

Wine related items for sale? Yes
Picnic area? Yes
Food available? Light snacks
Special Programs? Seminars, wine dinners
Facilities for private functions? Yes

Owners: Whitie and Margaret Hubert

Riverfront is what Whitie and Margaret Hubert wanted when they were looking for a place to retire. The 475-acre farm in Loudoun County that they purchased in 1985 has over three-quarters of a mile of it. When the Potomac flooded only two months after they closed on the property, they probably thought they'd gotten more river than they bargained for. As it turned out, the flood solved the problem of what to name the farm. Remembering the spot where Noah's ark had finally come to rest, a family member suggested Ararat. Fortunately for those of us whose tongues stumble over the name of the biblical mount, the Huberts turned it around and called their place Tarara.

"People tell us," says Margaret, "that we spell it backwards because we soon found out we didn't come here to retire—we came to work!" One of the first things Whitie did in his new home was to plant grapes—six rows of twelve varieties next to the farmhouse the Huberts were living in at the time. By 1987 he had decided that corn and soybeans were out and nursery stock and wine grapes were in. There are now seventy acres of ornamental trees and shrubs and fifty acres of vines.

The winery at Tarara is on a bluff overlooking the Potomac River. On the other side are the state of Maryland and Sugarloaf Mountain. You can see them after climbing the stairs to the wide deck in front of the tasting room, which is built into the side of the wooded cliff. At the entrance, stone retaining walls and winding stairs leading to a stone parapet create the impression that you're about to enter the hall of the mountain king. The lighting inside is subdued, in keeping with the subterranean mood. Here you'll be poured traditional vinifera varietals and blends surrounded by the colorful, modernistic paintings of one of the Huberts' daughters and the beautiful and artistic basketry of another. Sumptuously carved wooden wall panels with wine motifs in relief are the commissioned work of an artist in Luca, Italy.

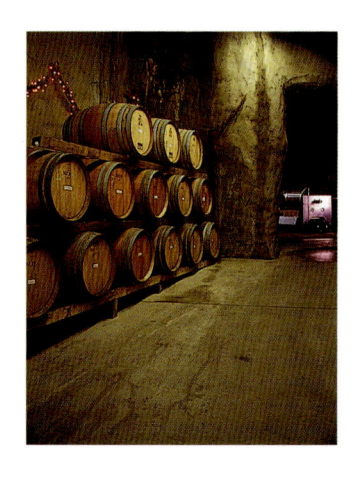

Tarara's current annual output is around 7,000 cases, and here the winemaker has full responsibility not only for the wines but for the vineyards as well—an enviable situation from the point of view of the viniculturist. Tarara currently sells a significant portion of their harvest to other Virginia wineries, but growth plans call for a doubling of capacity and eventual use of most of the grapes they grow in their own wines.

Several innovations at Tarara are aimed at increasing efficiency, without ever losing sight of the issue of quality. As an example, with grapes that can be destemmed and crushed quickly after harvesting, each of the workers picks into a single plastic lug, which, when full, is immediately emptied into one of three half-ton bins on a tractor-pulled trailer. This replaces the more labor-intensive—and lug-intensive—method of picking into separate lugs and lining them up along the rows, to be stacked on a trailer one by one after the picking is done and later unloaded and emptied—again one by one. At the winery, a forklift transfers an entire bin-load of grapes into the crusher/destemmer at one time.

Tarara is producing a list of about fifteen wines, including dry whites—like Pinot Gris, Chardonnay, and Viognier—and the red Bordeaux varietals. Dry and semi-dry blends like *Dry River Red* and *Terra Rouge* make reference to two important factors affecting conditions in the vineyards—the proximity of the Potomac River, and the soil. To satisfy your sweet palate, *Wild River Red* is vinted from estate-grown blackberries and blended with Chambourcin and Vidal Blanc.

After sampling them in the tasting room, you'll be eager to see where these outstanding wines are being made. The way to the winery and cellar is clearly indicated on a door to the left of the bar with a plaque that reads simply, "Cave." Once you've passed through, you'll be in a 230-foot-long, man-made tunnel that is twenty feet high and thirty feet wide, with stainless steel tanks flanking you on either side as you descend the ramp and voices ricocheting off the walls. The press is stationed at about the half-way point, by the double doors that swing open onto the crush pad. Barrels occupy most of the rest of the underground chamber. Whitie Hubert is retired from his own commercial construction business. If he happens to be giving the tour, you'll get a detailed account of what's involved in creating a cave this size out of solid rock.

For those who fancy the idea of spending the night in a winery, Tarara's bed and breakfast is built directly above the tasting room and the cellars and is intimately connected with both in a maze of stairways and passageways that is truly ingenious, not to mention intriguing. Polished granite floors and bare wood ceilings in the common areas unite with stone fireplaces and glass exterior walls in a way that marries small inn comfort with grand hotel luxury. In each room a unique winery welcome awaits you in a complimentary bottle of wine from the cellar and, when they're in bloom, long-stemmed roses from the vineyards.

Unicorn Winery

Unicorn Winery
487 Old Bridge Road
Amissville, VA 20106

Hours: 10 a.m. to 5 p.m. Saturday and Sunday. Closed on major holidays.

Directions: From **Warrenton,** take Rte. 211 west for 7 miles and turn right onto Rte. 622. Go 1 mile to the winery, on the right. From **Richmond,** take I-95 north to **Fredericksburg,** then Rte. 17 north to Rte. 29 north. Take first Warrenton exit (business Rte. 29), then Rte. 211 west for 7 miles to Rte. 622. Turn right and go 1 mile to the winery. From **D.C.,** take I-66 west to Rte. 29 south to Rte. 211 west. Go 7 miles to Rte. 622. Turn right and go 1 mile to the winery.

Phone: 540-347-7069
Website: www.unicornwinery.com

Tasting fee: None, except $1 per person for large groups

Wines: Chardonnay, Viognier, Seyval Blanc, Vidal Blanc, Chardonel, Chambourcin, Merlot, Cabernet Franc

Wine related items for sale? Yes
Picnic area? Yes
Food available? Light snacks
Facilities for private functions? Yes

Owner: David Whittaker
Winemaker: Chris Pearmund

Northern Region

The human subconscious is a vast desktop of memories and impressions, most of which, once set aside, become buried deeper and deeper under the accumulating pile, never to surface again. When the need arises, however, a little rummaging will occasionally turn up a useful bit of information from the past. When Dave Whittaker began thinking about what to call his new winery, his brain rather quickly returned the suggestion *Unicorn,* one that Dave immediately applauded. What kept him wondering was why he was so intrigued with the idea of naming his winery after this mythical creature. On the very day of the grand opening, June 10, 2000, his subconscious finally located the missing half of the memory.

The year was 1968 and Dave was in San Jose, California for three months, training for a position with IBM. While there he spent much of his free time touring wineries. The Irish Rovers had a hit at the time, a fanciful tune called "The Unicorn Song," that played over and over on the radio as Dave drove from one West Coast winery to the next.

He soon forgot about the Rovers and unicorns, but in the eighties, with Virginia's reinvented wine industry becoming more and more visible, Dave's interest in wineries was suddenly renewed as well. In 1988 he took a course in grape growing sponsored by Virginia Tech and conducted by the state's viticulturist, Dr. Tony Wolf. He also started looking for a vineyard site. He finally found one in 1993—on a sliver of Culpeper County wedged between Rappahannock and Fauquier Counties along the banks of the Rappahannock River. He began planting grapes the following year.

Dave, who worked for over twenty years troubleshooting IBM equipment, is something of a mechanical genius. This skill, coupled with a real aptitude for locating a bargain, has enabled him to construct and outfit his facility on a grass-roots-winery budget. Much of the winemaking equipment used in the first year of Unicorn's operation had been previously owned by another Virginia winery. The forty-by-eighty-foot steel frame building that now houses the production area and the Grape Barn, as the tasting room is called, lay in the path of major highway construction. Dave disassembled it himself and re-erected it at the vineyard. Now clad in lap siding and simply, but charmingly, decorated on the inside, the "barn" provides a cool and comfortable place to get to know Unicorn's owner and its wines. Flags from the major wine producing countries float from the ceiling, adding color and interest to an uncluttered interior.

In the summer of 1999, with his grapes maturing on the vine and no one to turn them into something people might enjoy drinking, Dave was feeling a bit uneasy about his first commercial crush. But some people do have all the luck, and on the advice of fellow winery owner Jim Law (Linden Vineyards), Dave called Chris Pearmund to see if he would be interested in the job of consulting winemaker. Chris is well known and highly regarded within the state's wine industry, not only for the top-quality grapes he produces in his own vineyards in Fauquier County, but also as a veteran—if still quite young—winemaker creating Virginia vintages of distinction for the past decade.

Using fruit from Dave's eight acres at the winery, as well as Chardonnay from his own vineyards, Seyval Blanc from rising star Breaux Vineyards, and others, Chris created a list of eight wines—from dry to sweet—with which to celebrate the opening of Unicorn Winery. The initial production was about 900 cases—small, to be sure, but in the space of a month, three of their varietals—the Viognier, the Merlot, and the Chambourcin—were on allocation, selling briskly without the benefit of a tasting.

Customers *were* able to taste Unicorn's debut Seyval, as well as its Chardonel, a hardy cross between the Seyval and the Chardonnay which does particularly well at Dave's somewhat frost-prone elevation of 525 to 550 feet. The Chardonnay was made from the same grapes—those from Chris's vineyard—that went into another Virginia winery's gold-medal winner in an international competition attracting over 1,100 Chardonnay entries. Unicorn's first-time *Vidal Reserve* contained Traminette (an offspring of the German Gewürztraminer) from the vineyard just outside the tasting room window.

The two-tiered deck Dave built next to the tasting room is completely shaded by trees in summer. The pond just beyond the railing on the lower level is an aquatic sports arena of vaulting bullfrogs and high-jumping bass. Tall-standing water lilies appear to surf the water in a gentle breeze. Picnic tables are plentiful—by the deck, in an open meadow across the pond, alongside the tree-lined avenue between the two vineyards at the front of the property. A walking path is planned that will lead past the vineyard down to the river and a recreation area with volleyball court and horseshoe pit.

If you feel you haven't learned enough about wines and winemaking by reading this far in this book, check out the rare tome in hard cover on display in Dave's tasting room. It's a compendium of everything one local wine enthusiast has learned about the subject. It's a fairly thick volume, but it's a quick read that will have you feeling like the consummate wine pro before you've finished the first chapter.

Willowcroft Farm Vineyards

Willowcroft Farm Vineyards
38906 Mount Gilead Road
Leesburg, VA 20175

Hours: 11 a.m. to 5 p.m. Friday, Saturday, and Sunday from March through December; weekends only during February. By appointment only in January. Closed Thanksgiving, Christmas, and December 31.

Directions: From **D.C.,** take Rte. 267 (Dulles Toll Road) to Leesburg. Take Rte. 15 south towards Warrenton. Go 2.5 miles and turn right onto Rte. 704 (Harmony Church Road) then immediately left onto Rte. 797 (Mount Gilead Road). Go 3.1 miles to the winery, on the right. If coming **from the south, on Rte. 15,** approximately 6 miles north of Gilbert's Corner, turn left onto Rte. 651 then left onto Rte. 797 and go 1 mile to the winery, on the right.

Phone: 703-777-8161
Fax: 703-777-8157
E-mail: willowine@aol.com
Website: www.willowcroftwine.com

Tasting fee: None, except $2 per person for groups of 10-25

Wines: Chardonnay, Riesling, Seyval Blanc, Vidal Blanc, Merlot, Cabernet Sauvignon, Cabernet Franc, *Applause* apple wine

Wine related items for sale? Yes
Picnic area? Yes
Food available? Light snacks

Owner: Lew Parker
Winemaker/Viticulturist: Lew Parker

A beneficent Providence, foreseeing the eventual revival of Virginia's wine industry, has seen fit to strew potential vineyard sites across the state with an abundant supply of old barns, a type of structure that is readily converted to winery purposes. Hill barns are especially adaptable since they come with built-in insulation on three sides.

According to owner Lew Parker, the red bank barn at Willowcroft was probably built shortly after the Civil War, possibly on the stone foundation of an earlier one. Chances that it predates the war are slim; during the month of December 1864 Union troops burned every barn they could find in Loudoun County, on the northernmost border of the Confederacy.

Lew got into the winemaking business purely by accident. In 1979 he purchased thirty acres on a mountaintop so that his daughters, who were enthusiastic 4-H members, would have some place to carry out their experiments in small animal husbandry. "Somewhere along the way," he says, "I discovered that it was hypothetically possible to grow vinifera grapes in Virginia." A year after buying the property, Lew planted his first vines, and in 1984 he pressed his first vintage. There are now 3½ acres at the winery site. Another eleven, at other vineyards on the same mountain, are under long-term lease.

Willowcroft currently produces about 2,000 cases of wine a year and regularly sells its excess grapes to other Virginia producers. There will be less fruit for sale over the next few years, however, as Lew gradually increases his own production. A recent expansion in the winery proper has resulted in a doubling of capacity, which will still keep Willowcroft in the small winery category—a place where Lew intends to remain.

Willowcroft's oaked wines are aged in a new, climate-controlled barrel room—an extension of the original underground production area that had once been quarters for livestock. Lew uses only American-made barrels. "We've never used French barrels," he says. "We like the flavor of the American oak. We started out using it and just never changed over."

Tastings are conducted on the ground floor over the winery. A row of horse stalls runs along one side where you enter through the barn doors. From the center aisle you can see into the hayloft—a wide, open space above the hallway. The tasting room is in the former tack room, under the loft. Wines you'll sample here are usually poured by Lew's wife, Amy, who handles the retail and marketing aspects of the family-run enterprise, and they include traditional vinifera and French hybrid varietals. Their *Cold Steel* Chardonnay is fermented in the manner implied in its name, while the reserve edition has the butter and toasted oak characteristics of a traditional barrel-fermented Chardonnay. The winter of 1996 was particularly severe on Virginia's vineyards, and that autumn Lew found himself extremely short of grapes. In order to have something to sell, he made apple wine—for the first time—from locally grown fruit. Willowcroft's *Applause* is a delicious off-dry stand-in wine that has become a perennial favorite on the list.

The drive up the slopes of Mount Gilead to the winery is 3½ miles long, but the view when you get there is well worth

the trek. From the picnic area in the meadow next to the winery, you can see into beautiful Loudoun Valley and beyond it the very ancient and very serene Blue Ridge Mountains. Where Mount Gilead drops off just a few feet from your table, the ground is covered with crown vetch, a delicate pink wild flower with a subtle come-hither fragrance. Bees are attracted to it, and every year the Parkers rent hives and sell honey in the tasting room—honey made at least in part from crown vetch nectar.

Lew and Amy live just a few yards from the winery in a rambling, wood-frame farmhouse whose core is a log cabin built circa 1790. The weeping willows in their yard are the source of the winery's name. The barn is directly behind the house through the stone gate at the end of the winding driveway.

Like many Virginia winegrowers, Lew has recently had to install a deer fence at the winery vineyard to protect his grapes from raids, in broad daylight sometimes, by these four-legged croplifters. The Parkers host special wine tastings and food and wine pairings throughout the year. One of the best attended is the venison and red wine sampling in March. Any deer who may still be thinking of attempting to trespass in Willowcroft's vineyards should be warned: the winery calendar makes a point of emphasizing that the venison for this event comes "from *our* woods."

Deer Meadow Vineyard

Deer Meadow Vineyard
199 Vintage Lane
Winchester, VA 22602

Hours: 11 a.m. to 5 p.m. Wednesday through Sunday and most Monday holidays from March through December.

Directions: From **Rte. 50 west of Winchester,** go south on Rte. 608 for 6.5 miles. Turn left onto Rte. 629 then right onto Vintage Lane. From **Rte. 55 west of I-81,** turn north onto Rte. 600, which becomes Rte. 608, and go 8 miles to Rte. 629. Turn right and go 1 mile to Vintage Lane, on the right. From the **D.C.** area, take I-66 west to Rte. 81 south to Rte. 55 west and follow the directions above for Rte. 55. From **Harrisonburg,** take I-81 north to Rte. 55 west and follow the directions above for Rte. 55.

Phone: 540-877-1919 or 800-653-6632
E-mail: dmeadow@shentel.net

Tasting fee: None

Wines: Chardonnay, *Golden Blush, Afternoon of the Fawn,* Chambourcin

Wine related items for sale? Yes
Picnic area? Yes

Owners: Charles and Jennifer Sarle
Winemakers/Viticulturists: Charles and Jennifer Sarle

For thirty years the land that Charles and Jennifer Sarle owned in the Shenandoah Valley near Winchester was called simply "the farm." The glade which they could see from their kitchen window, however, always had a name—Deer Meadow—and it was seldom that they would look out and not see at least one white-tailed deer that had ventured out of the surrounding woods into the open. When they needed a name for their winery, the choice was easy.

One thing you can't fail to notice when you visit Deer Meadow is that you are very far out in the country. As the climbing, winding dirt road breaks out of the woods, meadows on either side offer views of several mountain ranges. On an especially clear day, Massanutten and the Blue Ridge are layered against the horizon in receding shades of blue, while the Alleghenies can be seen spiking the sky along Virginia's western rim. There are coyotes up here, according to Jennifer, and grouse for them to try to catch. At night, two tiny lights in the distance are the only evidence of other human life.

Charles and Jennifer always wanted to grow grapes, but it was not until early retirement allowed them to leave their jobs in Indiana that they were able to come back to the farm and start their vineyard. They planted five acres in 1983 and currently have eight. Varieties include Cabernet Sauvignon, Maréchal Foch, Chambourcin, Steuben, and Chardonnay. Jennifer would like to add Vidal because the skins are tough and hard for birds to get into. These grapes also ripen late, and she's heard that deer tend to leave them alone. An eight-foot-high fence has proven to be the best solution for protecting those varieties that the deer seem to favor.

At an elevation of more than 1,100 feet, thermal inversion and a late bud break usually protect the Sarles's crop from spring frost damage. On rare occasions a hard spring freeze can, however, destroy entire plants. As Charles explains it, when the weather starts to warm, the sap begins to rise, filling the trunk. A sudden drop in temperature that is much below thirty-two degrees will freeze the sap, causing it to expand and split open the vine.

Charles, whose background is in mechanical engineering, designed and built the winery himself. The two-story construction is located on an incline and employs a gravity-flow system for handling the grapes during crush. Crushing and pressing take place on the upper level outside the cold room, where grapes of the same variety are temporarily stored at harvest until the entire crop can be picked. Oak barrels and stainless steel tanks are on the ground level. From the barrel room visitors ascend a circular stairway to the tasting room. The steps are made of solid ash and are supported by a center post consisting of a single, hand-barked cedar tree. A pair of Alaskan caribou antlers greets you as you round the corner at the top of the stairs.

Annual production at this mountain winery is 800 cases. With one exception, Deer Meadow produces only varietals, and these are all dry. Their *Golden Blush* is made from the Steuben, an American hybrid. It's a red variety which the Sarles process like white grapes so that only minimal color is extracted from the skins. *Blanc de noir* is the French term—literally, white from black (meaning red) grapes. The Sarles gave the wine its name, *Golden Blush,* because of the changes that occur while it's being made. When the grapes are pressed, the must has a beautiful pink, or blush, complexion. During fermentation the color changes to peach, and aging brings on its clear, golden tones. The Steuben also gives the color to *Afternoon of the Fawn,* which blends this American grape with French hybrid varieties to yield a slightly sweet wine with 2 percent residual sugar.

After you've sampled Charles and Jennifer's wines, you needn't be in a hurry to get back to the city. There's a tasting room deck on Charles's drawing board. In the meantime, at the man-made pond just a few yards farther down the slope you can fish, have a picnic lunch, or just sit and reflect on your surroundings in this designated wildlife sanctuary in the heart of Virginia's wilderness. If you're in a more secluded frame of mind, there's a path in Upper Meadow leading to an overlook and a nice view of the winery and vineyards below.

It's peaceful at Deer Meadow but not necessarily quiet. A pair of fast-trotting, free-range guineas are apt to be kicking up a fowl ruckus, and the bell you'll ring to summon the proprietors is an auditory experience all its own. The roosters run in packs here, and in the middle of the day you can hear their crowing, a definitively rural sound that is truly sublime at any time—except perhaps at five in the morning.

Landwirt Vineyard

Landwirt Vineyard
8223 Simmers Valley Road
Harrisonburg, VA 22802

Hours: 1 p.m. to 5 p.m. Saturday and Sunday from April through December. By appointment only from January through March.

Directions: From **I-81,** take exit 257 and go south on Rte. 11 for 2 miles. Turn right onto Rte. 806 and go 2.5 miles. At the intersection of Rtes. 806 and 619, go straight for .8 miles to the winery, on the right. From **Richmond** and **Charlottesville,** take I-64 west to I-81 north towards Harrisonburg and follow the directions for I-81 above. From the **D.C.** area via I-66 west, take I-81 south towards Harrisonburg and follow the directions for I-81 above.

Phone: 540-833-6000
E-mail: landwirt@shentel.net
Website: www.valleyva.com/landwirt.html

Tasting fee: None

Wines: Chardonnay, Riesling, Pinot Noir, Cabernet Franc, Cabernet Sauvignon, *Gewchardignon.*

Owner: Gary W. Simmers
Winemaker/Viticulturist: Gary Simmers

Shenandoah Valley Region

It's not easy keeping up with tall Gary Simmers as he strides up and down the length of his winery, but the pace of the tour is brisk when the guide is busy racking Chardonnay. On a Sunday afternoon in June, you could find Gary pumping the clear, finished wine from the oak barrels where it has been lying *sur lies* (on the sediments) for the last nine months into a stainless steel holding tank. If the regular winery help is not around, you might be asked to move a hose or to just step aside, and satisfactory performance of either duty could earn you a promotion from mere onlooker to temporary cellar master.

Getting this close to the actual winemaking is unusual for a visitor to a Virginia winery, even a smaller one, but it is typical of the informal style that permeates the Landwirt operation. In the very compact tasting room you'll sit at a plain kitchen table, and if your group is quite small, the winemaker may sit down with you while you sample varietals made from the seven kinds of vinifera grapes currently planted. "We're country folks who enjoy having people around," he'll tell you between pours. "Our intent is to get to know our customers, keep in contact with them, and become their personal vintners."

Gary, who has an engineering degree from Virginia Tech, is a third-generation farmer in Simmers Valley, and he remembers when every house for two miles in both directions along Simmers Valley Road was occupied by a family with the same name as his. Now he's the last. "I've gone from farming 600 acres before to farming 14 acres of grapes. It takes as much time for those 14," he says, "as it did for 600. Ninety percent of the effort goes into the vineyard." The rest goes into turning the fruit of his vines into first-rate wines, labels that won seventeen medals their first time out of the gate. That was in 1996, when the winery opened, for his 1995 vintage. Before that other wineries had been taking home golds for wines made with Landwirt grapes planted as far back as 1982.

The vineyards are at 1,200 to 1,300 feet on terroir that is volcanic rock and chert. The former dairy farm has at least another 100 acres that Gary feels are ideal for growing grapes. Expansion is definitely on his mind, including either a facelift for the current building or upgrade to a completely new winemaking and hospitality facility. If it's the latter, everything will be relocated to a site he and wife Teresa have picked out on the top of a hill with a rapture-inducing view of three mountain ranges: Massanutten and the Blue Ridge to the east and the Alleghenies to the west. Up here you can see all the way to New Market Gap and into West Virginia, certainly one of the most expansive views at any winery in the Old Dominion.

Landwirt is currently producing 3,500 cases of wine a year in a long, narrow, solid oak and block building, a retrofitted chicken house that attests to the diverse agricultural heritage of this multi-generational farm. "For making wine I couldn't ask for anything more," says Gary. "But outside," he thinks, "it leaves something to be desired." Repeat customers from as far away as New York think it leaves nothing to be desired but that he and Teresa will not be out of any of their wines—including the unique and delightful blend of Gewürztraminer, Chardonnay, and Sauvignon Blanc which they have whimsically named *Gewchardignon*, with scant regard for the easily tongue-tied.

With the above exception, Gary does very little blending at his winery, preferring to vint mostly dry, 100 percent varietals. His Chardonnay, however, is a blend of sorts in that he makes it from four different lots fermented with four different strains of yeast to create a very complex wine. To ensure the proper balance of oak in the finished product, prior to bottling he cuts his Chardonnay, if necessary, with wine that has been fermented and aged entirely in stainless steel. "You can spend a lifetime learning about wine," says Gary, who is mostly self-taught in the art, "and the variety and the options are endless."

Those who speak it will recognize Landwirt as the German word for farmer, or "caretaker of the land." Gary, whose family originally came from Germany—as did so many who settled the Shenandoah Valley—gave his place its name on the advice of two exchange students from the German-speaking region of Switzerland. "It carried over to the vineyard and winery," he explains, "and ties into the farm winery concept nicely. This is the farmer's winery and I am the farmer."

At this winery you'll get a clear sense of the sheer labor that goes into coaxing from nature one of its nicest gifts. Look across the vineyards towards the mountains in the west. On a chilly October evening, twin peaks cradle a setting sun as it slips beneath a cloudy comforter. Sweet dreams of long hours on hot days, ripe grapes on heavy vines, and lovely wines on the list at Landwirt Vineyard.

North Mountain Vineyard & Winery

North Mountain Vineyard and Winery
4374 Swartz Road
Maurertown, VA 22644

Hours: 11 a.m. to 5 p.m. Wednesday through Sunday and federal holidays from March through November; Saturdays and Sundays from December through February. Groups accommodated by appointment. Closed Christmas and New Year's Day.

Directions: From **metro D.C.**, take I-66 west, then I-81 south for 10 miles to exit 291 (Toms Brook). Go west on Rte. 651 for 1.5 miles to Mt. Olive. Turn left onto Rte. 623 and go 2 miles. Turn left onto Rte. 655 and go .3 miles to Swartz Road. Turn right. Winery is .3 miles on the left.

Phone: 540-436-9463
E-mail: wine@northmountain-vineyard.com
Website: www.northmountain-vineyard.com

Tasting fee: None

Wines: Chardonnay, Riesling, Cabernet Sauvignon, Chambourcin, Claret, and *Spiced Apple*

Wine related items for sale? Yes
Picnic area? Yes
Food available? Light snacks
Facilities for private functions? Yes

Owners: the Foster-Jackson family
Winemaker: John Jackson

Shenandoah Valley Region

Designed to resemble a Scandinavian farmhouse, architecturally speaking this is one of the most enchanting small wineries in Virginia. In any season and from every perspective, you can't help wondering, Is this the Shenandoah Valley or the charmed setting for a Norwegian fairy tale?

It is certainly Virginia—and it is definitely spellbinding. The winery sits snugly in a little dell with vineyards traipsing up the hill in the front and open fields sunning themselves on the hill towards the back. Mountain ranges to the east and to the west comment silently on the scale of everything that's taking place down here in the valley.

The original ten acres of vines at North Mountain were planted in 1982 by its founder, Dick McCormack, and construction of the current facility was completed in 1989. Ownership of the winery changed hands in 1998 when John Jackson took over the operation.

John works full-time as a geologist for the federal government, but weekends find him at North Mountain, either in the vineyards or in the winery. John sees his avocation as winegrower and winemaker as a natural extension of his profession as a geologist. "Geology is very field oriented," he says, "and I enjoy working in the field. It's a very hands-on science." Growing grapes is hands on in the extreme, with long hours spent pruning vines and tying shoots, but there's much pleasure to be derived from the quiet solitude of the vineyard.

As a specialist in the X-ray analysis of rocks, John is also a lab person and tends to refer to his winery as his laboratory. "I'm one of those who feel winemaking is a scientific endeavor," he comments, noting that at least half of his colleagues in the industry would disagree. "With my background, when I look at wine, I look at the chemistry of it," he says, adding that he wants to balance that approach by starting to look more at the artistic side of winemaking as well.

John's aim at North Mountain is to build on the foundation established by Dick McCormack, his mentor and winery consultant. At the same time he'll be writing new chapters in the history of North Mountain with the development of his own style in the vineyards and in the winery. One of the changes he's already made is to bring in stainless steel tanks and oak barrels to replace the almost exclusively plastic fermentation and storage containers Dick used for making his wines. In the years to come, visitors can expect more oak and more age from the wines they sample at John's winery. The five-year plan also calls for an increase in production from the current 1,200 annual cases to between 3,000 and 5,000 cases.

John's partners in his winemaking enterprise are his mother and step-father, Krista and Brad Foster, who have opted to sell their small resort business in Texas and move to Virginia to help their son. When the job descriptions have all been finalized, John will be spending most of his time in the winery, and Brad's responsibilities will lie primarily in the vineyards. Krista, whose strengths are in marketing, retailing, and administration, will be taking care of those phases of the operation.

During the War Between the States battles were fought up and down the Shenandoah Valley as the Union army sought to secure a possible invasion route into the North and gain control of one of the Confederacy's most vital agricultural regions. Stonewall Jackson was in charge of thwarting the aims of the Federal troops, and his string of Southern victories in the spring and summer of 1862 were exuberantly celebrated as Jackson's Valley campaign. The tide turned, however, in 1864 when Philip Sheridan swept through with orders from General Grant to take the Valley once and for all. At the Battle of Tom's Brook, just a few miles from North Mountain, the Confederates recognized the need to withdraw (John cannot bring himself to use the word *retreat*). In what would later be called the Woodstock Races, they withdrew south in great haste towards Woodstock, coming down Swartz Road right across the present-day winery property. The skirmish that ensued when Union troops caught up took place on land adjacent to John's vineyards.

North Mountain Winery beckons visitors with a tradition of award-winning wines from Cabernets and Chardonnays to an enticing dry apple wine that tastes and smells just like fresh apple pie. A second-story event room is available for private functions and also serves as a gallery where the paintings of local artists are displayed. The deck off the tasting room and the picnic area it overlooks invite your lingering participation in the beauty and tranquility of the surroundings. Add to this the richness of the area's history and tourists contemplating a sweep of the Shenandoah wineries will do well to make the visit to John Jackson's an extended expedition in their own campaign through the Valley.

Shenandoah Vineyards

Shenandoah Vineyards
3659 S. Ox Road
Edinburg, VA 22824

Hours: 10 a.m. to 6 p.m. daily from March through November; 10 a.m. to 5 p.m. December through February. Guided tours on the hour beginning at 11 a.m. Closed on Thanksgiving, Christmas, and New Year's Day.

Directions: From **I-81,** take exit 279 at Edinburg. Go west on Stoney Creek Road. Turn right onto S. Ox Road. Winery is 1.5 miles on the left. From **Richmond** and **Charlottesville** via I-64 west, take I-81 north towards Harrisonburg and follow directions above. From **D.C.** via I-66 west, take I-81 south towards Harrisonburg and follow the directions for I-81 above.

Phone: 540-984-8699
Fax: 540-984-9463
E-mail: shenvine@shentel.net
Website:
www.shentel.net/shenvine

Tasting fee: None

Wines: Cabernet Sauvignon, Merlot, Chambourcin, Riesling, Chardonnay

Wine related items for sale? Yes
Picnic area? Yes
Food available? Light snacks
Facilities for private functions? Yes

Owner: Emma Randel
Winemaker: Rick Burroughs

Not only is Shenandoah the name of a valley, a river, a mountain range, a great movie starring Jimmy Stewart, and the fifth oldest winery in Virginia, it also designates the largest winegrowing region—geographically speaking—in the state. Viticultural appellations are federally approved, and this one actually climbs the slopes of the Alleghenies and topples over into West Virginia, encompassing mountain and valley terrain deemed especially suitable for growing wine grapes. The Shenandoah appellation resulted from the efforts of the late Jim Randel—co-founder along with his wife, Emma, of Shenandoah Vineyards—and stretches up the Valley from the northern tip of Virginia south to the James River just north of Roanoke.

In 1974, after Jim suffered a heart attack, he and Emma came down from their home in New Jersey to spend time on her family farm near Edinburg. An article in a regional magazine about growing wine grapes in Virginia sparked Jim's interest, and in 1976, Emma—with the help of their five children, their children's friends, and other relatives—planted 5,000 French hybrid vines on eight acres behind the barn on the Blue Ridge side. Emma herself walked behind the tree planter—stamping the earth around each and every vine to eliminate any air pockets. Two years later the Randels planted another eight acres, this time in front of the barn on the Massanutten side, and this time mainly in viniferas.

Altogether Shenandoah now has approximately thirty-five acres of vines at this and other properties it owns or controls close by. Because they're on the western side of the Blue Ridge Mountains, most varieties tend to bud out later here than in the rest of the state. That means little frost damage for winegrowers in this region, because by the time bud break occurs, the late spring frosts have usually come and gone. It's interesting to note that in an area of Virginia heavily settled by Germans during the 1700s, the Riesling—a German variety that often poses problems for growers in other parts of the state—tends to do better here in the slightly milder, cooler microclimates of the Shenandoah Valley.

Since 1985 Emma has been managing operations at Shenandoah, with the help of a small and dedicated staff. The winery is open seven days a week, and Emma is usually here six out of the seven. This petite winegrower with silver hair and sparkling blue eyes often conducts the tours herself. Her presentation of the winemaking process from vineyard to crush to bottling is succinctly informative, besides being entertaining and interactive. Your questions are welcome, and don't be surprised if Emma has a question or two for you as well. While in her company your curiosity will be satisfied regarding the blue plastic cylinders seen here and in other vineyards around the state. They're growing tubes for young vines—mini-hothouses, Emma calls them, for each new plant.

The cellar is under the tasting room in this Civil War-era bank barn turned winery. The dimly lit wine dormitory is wall to wall French and American oak tightly filling the spaces between very old hand-hewn timbers supporting the floor above. Down here you'll learn that—besides a gradual depletion of chemicals in the wood that give barrel-aged wines their special oaky characteristics—the useful life of a barrel is further shortened by tartaric acid crystals formed in the wine which eventually clog the pores of the wood, preventing it from releasing the remaining phenols. Red wines, Emma reminds you, generally cost more than white wines because they usually spend more time in the barrel, keeping the winemaker's investment in both wine and wood tied up for a longer period.

A room-sized vintage oriental rug covers the wide floor boards of the spacious tasting room at Shenandoah, and antique cabinets, cupboards, and hutches display a wide range of wine-related gifts. Working the sales room is the best part of owning a winery for Emma because here she gets to meet people who have come to the Valley from all over the world.

A review of winemaker Rick Burroughs' wines as conducted by Emma is a lesson in the right way to taste and how to employ all five senses while doing so. At her bar you're asked to take at least two sips, because the true flavors of any wine are revealed on the second pass. Selective pairing of food and wine can greatly enhance the flavors of both. To demonstrate, Emma will offer you a small piece of cheese with the *Shenandoah Ruby,* a lightly oaked proprietary red. They break with the Cabernet contingent at this winery by suggesting chocolate fudge with *Sweet Serenade,* a blend of several *white* grape varieties.

Before you taste, swirling the wine by gliding the base of the glass in tight circles on the counter top helps release its bouquet, treating your nose to the first impressions of a skilled winemaker's craft. A red varietal's age is partially revealed in the way it feels in your mouth, with older vintages generally creating softer tannic sensations than younger offerings from the same vineyard. Color says something about age as well. Emma can show you how a young wine's stronger color spreads evenly to the sides of the glass, while that of an older one appears to retreat from the edges, concentrating itself in the center of the glass.

Hearing is often overlooked when describing the sensory delights of a good wine, but the cheerful clinking of glasses, Emma reminds the visitor, is but another entry in the list of wine's enjoyments. And let's not forget the sound of laughter and the lively conversation of friends and relatives gathered round the table—or these same things shared with strangers come together from around the world at Emma Randel's bar.

Château Morrisette

Château Morrisette
287 Winery Road
Floyd, VA 24091

Hours: 10 a.m. to 5 p.m. Monday through Thursday; 10 a.m. to 8 p.m. Friday and Saturday; 11 a.m. to 5 p.m. on Sunday. Closed Thanksgiving, Christmas Eve, Christmas Day, and New Year's Day.

Directions: From the **Blue Ridge Parkway** at milepost 171.5, turn west onto Rte. 726 (Black Ridge Road) and make an immediate left onto Winery Road. Winery is 1/4 mile on the right.

Phone: 540-593-2865
Fax: 540-593-2868
E-mail: info@chateaumorrisette.com
Website: www.chateaumorrisette.com

Tasting fee: $1 per person; $2 per person for groups of 10 or more

Wines: Cabernet Sauvignon, Cabernet Franc, Merlot, Pinot Noir, Chardonnay, *Black Dog, Black Dog Blanc, Our Dog Blue, Blushing Dog, Sweet Mountain Laurel, Red Mountain Laurel*

Wine related items for sale? Yes
Picnic area? Yes
Food available? Light snacks from the deli; full-service restaurant
Special Programs? Wine Club

Owners: the Morrisette family
Winemaker: Dan Tallman
Viticulturist: Clyde Belcher

This family hobby turned family business began its public life as Woolwine Winery—named for a small town at the bottom of Rock Castle Gorge in rural Floyd County—on land belonging to founders William and Nancy Morrisette and their son David. But on top of sounding slightly redundant, the name was tricky for even the most agile tongue to negotiate, especially after a glass or two of Woolwine's wines. Besides, David wanted to know, where were the sheep to supply the wool for making wool wine? At his urging the name was soon changed to Château Morrisette.

What's in a name? Plenty, according to David, whose basic credo is that wine—making it, selling it, and drinking it—should be fun. Château Morrisette has risen from a small winery producing 2,000 cases in 1980 to become the state's second largest, with an annual case volume exceeding 55,000. Its rapid and steady growth has been fueled by the exceptional skills of its winemakers, of which David himself was the first, and a marketing acumen second to none. A prime example is *Our Dog Blue*. Originally put up in a brown bottle, this semi-sweet Riesling/Seyval blend was selling at the rate of 1,000 cases a year until David and then winemaker Bob Burgin gave it a catchy name and bottled it in blue. Sales soared higher than the cute little beagle for which it was named—depicted on the new label cheerfully leaping over the moon.

Blue was preceded by two other wines in what David calls their dog portfolio. *The Black Dog* (*Le Chien Noir* in the language of David's French Huguenot ancestors) is undisputedly Château Morrisette's most widely recognized label, although many consumers do not realize that the *chien* and the *château* are connected. It's an off-dry blend of Cabernet Sauvignon, Merlot, and Chambourcin that customers can't seem to get enough of. Originally called *Trilogy*, like *Our Dog Blue*, this wine skyrocketed to new sales heights when christened with its new *nom de vin*. Its companion wine, *Black Dog Blanc*, is an off-dry combination of Chardonnay, Seyval Blanc, and Vidal Blanc. While these two wines are of mixed varieties, the bloodlines of the canines who inspired them are pure black Labrador retriever. Hans—belonging to David—and his female companion, Be (Be still, Be quiet, and Behave!)—belonging to now vice-president Bob Burgin—

were the original Black Dogs, and they appear, vis-a-vis, on the winery's crest. Sadly, both Hans and Be have passed on. These days Nicholas Morrisette and the lady Jazz Burgin hold court at the château as the winery mascots.

A touch of Merlot added to the semi-dry blend of Seyval, Vidal, and Riesling brings the color to the cheeks of *Blushing Dog,* a wine that had wandered off the list for several years but happily has come back home again.

Off-dries, semi-sweets, and sweets make up the better part of Château Morrisette's list, but, says David, "we have a wine for every consumer who walks through the door. If they drink wine, we've got one for them." And those who prefer theirs fermented to complete dryness do not go begging. Classic, distinguished, barrel-aged varietals head the list: Chardonnay, Merlot, Cabernet Sauvignon, and more. In the year 2000, David started putting pictures of the Black Dog on his premium varietals, the first portrait being of Nicholas, the second of Jazz, and the third of the Labrador couple together. With the commencement of this practice Château Morrisette's labels have gone almost entirely to the dogs.

The exceptions, for now, are their very popular dessert wines, *Red Mountain Laurel* and *Sweet Mountain Laurel,* named for the indigenous shrub that flourishes in the Blue Ridge and can be seen blooming along the parkway in early to mid June. While the red contains a sizable component of Chambourcin for the color, both are made primarily from the Niagara—often referred to as "the white Concord"—a variety widely grown in upstate New York. This American vine handles extreme cold handily, and close to twenty acres of it thrive at the winery's altitude of nearly 3,500 feet, where it has replaced virtually every other grape the Morrisettes have attempted to grow this high up. Another twenty acres of vinifera find the environment much more hospitable farther down the mountain near Woolwine, at an elevation of about 1,600 feet. In addition to their own vineyards, the Morrisettes have contracts with over twenty other winegrowers throughout the state, bringing their total assured acreage to about 250.

The Blue Ridge Parkway being a parkway, there are no commercial signs along the winding, two-lane mountain road to guide you to Château Morrisette, not even the comforting red and green grape-cluster markers to reassure you that you're still on the right track. As you get very close, however, a plain sign in a field some distance from the highway announces simply, "Winery." As you approach the property along the access road, you soon realize that sign is a modest piece of advertising indeed.

The original "château" is the first thing you see. With an exterior constructed entirely of native stone from the Morrisette property, it stretches in mottled hues of blue and gray and brown across the far side of a meticulously kept lawn. This building, which has undergone a number of expansions, originally housed the winery, the tasting room, and, later, the restaurant. It is now devoted entirely to fine dining. There are two separate dining rooms. The newer one is broad and long and airy, with lattice windows at one end

Château Morrisette

and a view of the deck and beyond. The older one wraps you comfortably in dark paneling and subdued light and opens onto the front porch. Dinner patrons choosing to dine outside on the deck are treated to often lavish mountain sunsets behind rolling green hills.

Across the parking lot is the new winery and tasting room, a splendid structure completed in 1999 and taking 2½ years to build. According to David, it is the largest *salvaged* timber-frame building ever erected in the United States, and the interior is quite simply awe-inspiring. The two-story production and barrel-storage area is enormous. Its ceiling is a fretwork of crossbeams and arches made from eighty-five-year-old Douglas fir timbers reclaimed from the Saint Lawrence seaways, where they formed "floating sidewalks" for moving freshly felled Canadian logs down the waterways in an orderly fashion. Huge beams from an old warehouse somewhere on the docks in Seattle provided the timber framing for the tasting room and the raw materials for the exquisite vaulting in the great hall directly overhead.

The crush pad at Château Morrisette offers a unique opportunity for visitors during harvest. A wooden railing divides the pad into two areas. Tables and chairs on one side provide a place to sit and enjoy one of the winery's earlier vintages while watching the current one being crushed and pressed. The new twenty-two-ton press outside on the big concrete slab can process an entire tractor trailer load of grapes at one time.

David has a degree in viticulture and enology from Mississippi State and while a student there actually worked at the small winery owned by fellow student Bob Burgin. Ten years ago he persuaded his former classmate and employer to come on board as Château Morrisette's winemaker. Together the two friends have formulated a mission for the winery that aims to make wine accessible and unintimidating. Despite the imposing architecture, the atmosphere at this winery is relaxed and unaffected.

At one time or another David has worn all the hats at Château Morrisette, including that of gardener. It's not unusual to find him helping out at the garden center, where in spring and fall the winery sells many of the same flowers and plants that decorate the grounds. You may spot him just about anywhere, though; managing by walking around seems to be his style. Just keep an eye out for the black dog. His owner is sure to be somewhere close by.

115

Dye's Vineyards & Winery

Dye's Vineyards and Winery
Route 2, Box 357
Honaker, VA 24260

Hours: 1 p.m. to 9 p.m. daily except Sunday. Closed on Thanksgiving and Christmas.

Directions: Located approximately 1/4 mile from Rte. 80 on Rte. 620. **From Abingdon,** take Rte. 19 north to Rte. 80 west. Turn left onto Rte. 620. **From Bluefield, VA,** take Rte. 19 south to Rte. 80 west and turn left onto Rte. 620. **From Pikeville, KY,** take Rte. 80 east through Breaks Interstate Park. Turn right onto Rte. 620.

Phone: 540-873-4659
E-mail: cleody@yahoo.com
Website: www.geocities.com/eureka/suite/7435

Tasting fee: None

Wines: Vidal Blanc, Seyval Blanc, Villard Noir, De Chaunac, Cabernet Sauvignon, Chardonnay, Golden Muscat, *Richlands Red, Pink Vidal*

Wine related items for sale? Yes
Picnic area? Yes
Food available? Light snacks
Facilities for private functions? Yes

Owners: the Dye family
Winemaker/Viticulturist: John Dye

If you'd like to find out how they make wine in southwest Ohio, spend a little time at this winery in the far southwest corner of Virginia. Ken Dye grew up in Honaker, Virginia, where generations of his kin had farmed the tall, green hills—mini-mountains sprouting like bright new growth on the dark and ancient Appalachians. Ken left his native Russell County soon after graduating from high school and moved to Cincinnati, just a half day's journey across Kentucky. Here he rose from patrolman to chief of police in the suburb of Silverton. After retiring from the force and spending a few years on the town council, he returned to the ancestral farm in Virginia and began planting grapes.

Virtually all of the help Ken and wife Linda have received in their winemaking venture has come from people they know who are involved in the industry in Ohio. The first vines they put in the ground, in 1989 and 1990, were clippings of Vidal Blanc and De Chaunac they got from friends who own a winery in the Dyes' favorite American city. When he takes you on the tour of the cellar, one of the first things Ken wants you to know about this operation is that "everything you see in the winery that has to do with actually making wine came from Cincinnati." Indeed you will see some equipment here that is quite different from the norm at the rest of Virginia's wineries. The stainless steel fermentation tanks, for instance, are small, holding between 150 and 350 gallons, and are stacked in rows on their bellies like wooden barrels. Ken has also acquired some large culinary pots from a military surplus store. Used routinely at small Ohio wineries, they stand on four legs, waist high to an army cook. With their lids now welded shut and drilled with bung holes, they hold small lots of experimental wines or wines used mainly for blending.

Ken has been interested in wine and winemaking for most of his adult life. Although he's the founder and has made wine himself, according to Ken the real talent at Dye's Vineyards is his son John. Like his father, John Dye learned the art of winemaking in Cincinnati, where he began helping out in and around wineries as a young boy. His particular gift seems to be in coming up with just the right blend.

All of John's wines are chock full of flavor, and several of them provide very clear-cut examples of what is meant by a fruity, a floral, or a herbaceous nose. The Villard Noir and De Chaunac varietals, and the Vidal Blanc as well, exhibit the latter quite assertively. Villard Noir is a lesser known French hybrid that nonetheless has a strong following in Pennsylvania and, as you might suspect, Ohio. Even the novice enophile will easily recognize the grassy overtones—hints of new-mown hay drying in the sun—that lace this smooth, mighty well-mannered little red that just caresses your mouth with the softness of its tannins. The De Chaunac, another French hybrid, is already popular with many Virginia vintners. Ken considers their De Chaunac ideal for long-term aging. Despite its strong demand, with his '95 vintage he has begun the practice of holding back a small reserve for at least five years before this wine is finally bottled and released.

For a perfect understanding of what is meant by a fruity nose as opposed to a floral nose, try John's *Seyval Blanc* and his *Pink Vidal* blend, in that order. On second thought, since the subtleties of weather and the growing season in general make every vintage different from the one before, sample all their wines. You're bound to pick up obvious distinctions as you make your way down the list.

At present the Dyes are growing only French hybrid and American varieties. No vinifera have been planted yet, though they are vinifying a little Chardonnay and Cabernet Sauvignon from other Virginia vineyards. Their own grapes are planted on mountain terrain that seems to be nearly vertical, whether you're climbing the rocky hillside on your own foot power or using four-wheel drive. There are just four acres of vines here, separated down the middle by a narrow pasture that fans out above the vineyards to cover the side of the mountain at a higher elevation.

Having grown up on the mountain, Ken is intimately familiar with its microclimates. "When I was a boy and fed cattle all over this place," he says, "one of the warmest spots on the farm was where our vineyards are." Both he and Linda are pilots who understand air currents and air flow. "It flows just like water," says Ken, "only you can't see it. Above our vineyard you'll see spring frost come down almost to the vines." It will skip over the vineyard, he adds, and pick up again just below the log cabin where he was born. "There will be a band, a belt, where there won't be any frost at all," he says. "It's like being behind a waterfall," Linda explains. The cold air comes over the mountain like a river, cascading over the vineyard and splashing to earth again below it. "What you want to do in these mountains," says Ken, "is tuck your vineyard behind the waterfall."

The old log cabin, judiciously built in the hillside's frost-free band, has completely tumbled down. Something with a high-pitched, canine voice inhabits it now. Probably a coyote, Linda observes casually. At the top of the vineyard, the broad pasture behind it struggles up the mountain towards the tree line. In front, the view sweeps down across the vines towards the settlement below, then suddenly up again at more blue mountains patched with green fields. From down below comes the ring of a hammer, the sound of someone doing work the old-fashioned way. If this isn't the perfect picture of high-altitude agrarian Virginia, such a place doesn't exist.

In the late nineties Ken started the Far Southwest Virginia Vineyard Association. There are now more than twenty members, and Ken expects at least four or five small wineries like his to open in the next few years. He sees them not as competition but—by creating a sort of cluster effect—as actually bringing more visitors to his own establishment. In the meantime, a side trip to Break's Interstate Park or the historic town of Abingdon would round out an exceedingly pleasant visit to Dye's Vineyards. Other nearby attractions include the states of Kentucky and Tennessee.

Tomahawk Mill Winery

Tomahawk Mill Winery
9221 Anderson Mill Road
Chatham, VA 24531

Hours: 11 a.m. to 5 p.m. Tuesday through Saturday from March 15 through December 15, and by appointment. Closed Thanksgiving.

Directions: From **Business Rte. 29 in Chatham,** go west on Rte. 57 for 4.5 miles. Turn right onto Rte. 799 (Climax Road) and go 3.4 miles to Rte. 649 (Anderson Mill Road). Turn left and go 3 miles to the winery, on the left. From Rte. 40 east (after entering Pittsylvania County), turn right onto Rte. 626 (Museville Road) and go 7.4 miles to Rte. 649 (Anderson Mill Road). Turn left and go 2.5 miles to the winery, on the right.

Phone: 804-432-1063
Fax: 804-432-2037
E-mail: tomahawk@gamewood.net

Tasting fee: None, except $2 per person for groups of 10 or more. Fee is discounted from purchase.

Wines: Chardonnay, Riesling, Vidal Blanc, Concord (sweet and dry), apple wine, *Tobacco Road Blues, Earl of Chatham Mead*

Wine related items for sale? Yes
Picnic area? Yes
Food available? Light snacks
Facilities for private functions? Yes

Owners: Corky and Nancy Medaglia
Winemaker/Viticulturist: Corky Medaglia

There's probably nothing on the rural landscape that can stir up feelings of bucolic romanticism the way an old water-driven gristmill can. Mill wheels and millstones have about them idyllic auras rarely generated by other mechanical devices of such purely practical purpose.

The mill on Tomahawk Creek near Chatham was established in 1888 by James Anderson, a former Confederate soldier, and it continued to operate under the management of his descendants for 100 years. The last family member to own the corn and flour grinding business was Walter Crider, a kinsman of Anderson's on his mother's side. Walter had planted a small vineyard on an adjacent hill, and in 1988 he closed down the milling operation and two years later opened a small winery. Production was only 200 cases a year, a sideline winemaking enterprise intended to draw visitors to the historic mill. Walter had other farming operations to look after, and in 1996, in a move to "downsize," he sold the winery and mill, along with sixteen surrounding acres, to Corky and Nancy Medaglia.

Corky describes seeing the inside of the mill for the first time as somewhat like opening a time capsule: "Everything of an antique nature, particularly in the tasting room, was already here. It was as if the business was running full-swing one day and someone just closed and locked the door, leaving everything untouched."

The rough-sawn, unvarnished rusticity of the former office and sales room at this nineteenth-century place of business is what gives the tasting room of today its unique charm and special flavor. The sepia tones of the all-wood interior lend a daguerreotype quality and the feeling that you've stepped into a photograph of the past, where mortise and tenon joints, not nails, connect crossbeams and supporting timbers. Two flour sackers against the back wall are positioned under a pair of chutes that once gravity-fed milled wheat from the chamber above. For weighing the customer's purchase, there's an antique Franklin scale, an early American invention bearing patent number eleven. Photographs of the Anderson family on the wall remind you that this place once belonged to them.

Besides currently being the only vintner in Virginia selling wine out of a gristmill, Corky is the only one making his wine in a silo. Two former grain bins a few yards from the mill were converted by Walter Crider into a winery by the addition of concrete flooring and insulation and climate control. Corky is in the process of replacing Walter's plastic tanks with stainless steel. The new tanks are small, to fit into their somewhat cramped surroundings. On a typical weekend in June, you may find Corky fermenting *Earl of Chatham Mead,* a straight mead made strictly from honey and water that honors William Pitt, the earl of Chatham, for whom the nearby town was named. A tall visitor can look over the side and actually see the bubbling action taking place in the vat.

Production at Tomahawk Mill is up from Walter's 500 gallons a year to 1,500 gallons, or 600 cases. Wine is often made here in very small batches. It's not unusual to see a glass demijohn off to the side holding 14½ gallons—not quite six cases—of wine. Corky is also making Chardonnay and

Cabernet Sauvignon and aging them in French oak. After hand-bottling of these wines, the barrels are cleaned and filled with a sulfite solution to kill any yeast and bacteria and keep the wood from drying out until the barrels are needed again soon after crush.

Corky plans further increases in production but is presently operating close to capacity. There's a miller's house on the property that's almost as old as the mill itself. Corky wants to build a new winery next to it and perhaps turn the house into the tasting room. This contemplated shift in venue for wine sampling and sales is due to Corky's intention to once again start milling flour at Tomahawk Mill.

For a while Tomahawk Creek was diverted away from the mill while Corky worked on digging out the millpond to restore it to its original dimensions. In April of 2000 water once again flowed over the dam and into the millrace. The old water wheel is under the mill awaiting restoration. Corky thinks he has most of what he needs to get it up and turning, including replacement buckets and the original gear patterns, should he need them. Before too long the sight and sound of sheets of water cascading off the top of the mill wheel may once again delight the eyes and ears of visitors, adding another romantic dimension to the unique allure of Tomahawk Mill Winery.

Valhalla Vineyards

Valhalla Vineyards
6500 Mount Chestnut Road
Roanoke, VA 24018

Hours: Noon until 5 p.m. Saturday and 1 p.m. to 5 p.m. Sunday from May through June; noon to 4 p.m. Saturday and 1 p.m. to 4 p.m. Sunday from September through October.

Directions: From **I-81 at Roanoke**, take I-581 to Electric Road (Rte. 419). Go 2 miles on Rte. 419 and turn left onto Brambleton Avenue (Rte. 221), then 1 mile and turn right at the second stoplight onto Roselawn Road. Go 2.5 miles and turn left onto Mount Chestnut Road. Go 1 mile to the winery entrance, on the left.

Phone: 540-725-9463
Fax: 540-772-7858
E-mail: valhallava@aol.com
Website: www.valhallawines.com

Tasting fee: $2 per person (Includes large souvenir glass.)

Wines: Cabernet Sauvignon, Cabernet Franc, Syrah, Sangiovese, Chardonnay, Viognier, *Cornucopia*

Picnic area? Yes

Owners: Jim and Debra Vascik
Winemaker: Debra Vascik
Viticulturist: Jim Vascik

This winery performed the equivalent of a quadruple Axel when it entered the rink at the Virginia Governor's Cup competition in the year 2000. The contest turned into a showdown between Valhalla's 1998 Syrah and its 1998 Cabernet Franc, with the Syrah edging out its sibling rival to win the Cup, while the Franc skated away with second place honors. The icing on the victory cake for Valhalla was that the wines that won were from their first estate vintage, the winery having only opened its doors in 1998. Adding glitter to the icing was the fact that winemaker Debra Vascik became the first woman to win Virginia's most prestigious wine award.

Syrah has very little track record in Virginia. In terms of planted acreage this red vinifera from the Rhone Valley currently occupies a seat at the rear of the theater, while the red Bordeaux trio—the Cabernet twins and Merlot—take front and center stage. As a wine, however, Syrah is hardly shy and retiring. On the contrary, it's big and bold, the kind of wine Jim and Debra Vascik like to drink. So they ignored the cautions about planting this grape and allocated a small portion of their twenty-one planned acres to the variety which the Australians prefer to call Shiraz, after the city in ancient Persia where it is believed to have originated. At the time the Vasciks had no idea they were putting these vines into soils ideally suited for producing a truly remarkable wine.

According to Jim, the Rhone River Valley in southeast France is the best place in the world for growing Syrah. If you stand at the top of the overlook at Valhalla Vineyards, you will have a perfect view of what he describes as the Rhone Valley in Virginia. "It's the same view you get if you stand at the stone chapel in Hermitage," he says. "The only thing missing is the huge river flowing down the middle." Virginia's Roanoke River apparently compares to the Rhone like her James does to the mighty Mississippi. But, Jim continues, "they are at 2,000 feet; we are at 2,000 feet. They are on decomposing granite; we are on decomposing granite." While this may sound ominous—and imminent—keep in mind that Jim is talking about geology. This has been going on, and will continue to go on, for a very long time. The benefit to growers of Syrah is that the water trickling through and breaking up the granite leaches out minerals—nutrients—and the clefts created in the rock provide just enough maneuvering room for the tap root of this vine, which, Jim says, does best when it is severely stressed.

At Valhalla both the winery and the cellar are under the mountain. Arriving visitors actually drive over the cave, which is 200 feet long and slopes downward until its far end is sixty feet below the surface, directly under one of Valhalla's vineyards. The temperature in the cave hovers at a totally self-sustaining fifty-six to fifty-nine degrees year round, and the humidity stays at about 90 percent, ideal for aging and for minimizing the loss of wine through evaporation. The barrels lose only about an ounce a month, but Debra religiously tops them off every two weeks.

Indeed, extreme pampering of the grapes and the wines is the essence of Valhalla's style of winemaking. With the goal of creating world-class vintages from the start, Jim, who is a practicing physician, and Debra, who is a physical therapist, approached their foray into commercial winemaking by adopting what they considered to be the best practices of other wineries they had visited. Says Jim, "Everything we've done is basically copying other people. That's the sincerest form of flattery."

The kid-gloves treatment begins in the vineyards, where—after being picked early in the morning—Valhalla's grapes are sorted and immediately put into a refrigerated truck. On the roof of the winery, the reds are sorted once again, destemmed and crushed, and allowed to flow—with the help of gravity alone—into open-top tanks inside the cave. During a two-week fermentation period, Jim climbs up on the wooden catwalk three times a day to punch down the cap of skins and seeds that rises to the top. Every ounce of wine that goes into Debra's red varietals is from unpressed, free-run juice. "That's how I'm able to get such wonderful tannin balance," she says. The remaining wine that is pressed off the skins and seeds goes into separate barrels, tagged "P" for "pressed," and is used to create *Cornucopia,* a blended table wine softened by the addition of a little Chardonnay and up to eighteen months' aging in oak barrels.

The cave at Valhalla will hold roughly 350 barrels, upwards of 7,000 cases of wine, but the Vasciks have decided to limit production to between 4,500 and 5,000 cases a year. In Jim's words, that makes them boutique by California standards and small potatoes here in Virginia, something that doesn't bother him in the least. Five thousand cases is all he and Debra feel they can handle and still give the wines the attention they deserve. The business keeps four employees busy in the vineyards year round, and it's a full-time job for Debra as well. On any weekend you may find Jim in the winery dipping corked bottles of wine into a bubbling fondue pot, deftly applying the gold-toned wax seals they use in lieu of capsules on Valhalla's French-made, silk-screened bottles.

Meanwhile, Debra could be in the cave racking wine—transferring it from one barrel directly into another. Currently all Debra's wines are fermented to dryness, enabling her to bottle unfined and unfiltered, the method she prefers. She has plans for vinting a late harvest Viognier, a sweet dessert wine that will, therefore, require some filtering.

Being great fans of the music of Richard Wagner, Jim and Debra have named their winery and several of their wines after the grand themes of teutonic mythology celebrated in the German composer's operas. Valhalla is the hall of the god Odin into which the souls of those who have died bravely in battle are ushered by beautiful maidens called Valkyries—a name soon to be worn by a classic blend of Bordeaux reds under the Valhalla label. *Rheingold* is Debra's full-bodied, flinty reserve Chardonnay from a specific block in their vineyard, while her acclaimed Cabernet Franc is named for Wagner's sweeping opera *Götterdämmerung—*Twilight of the Gods.

It's strictly dawn, however—and a very promising one—at this earthly Valhalla. West Coast boutique or East Coast small potatoes, others will no doubt be looking to copy some of the practices that have created a flood of state, national, and international recognition for the wines being produced at this young but precocious Virginia winery.

Villa Appalaccia Winery

Villa Appalaccia Winery
Route 1, Box 661
Floyd, VA 24091

Hours: 11 a.m. to 5 p.m. Thursday and Friday, and 11 a.m. to 6 p.m. on Saturday from April through December.

Directions: Located just off the Blue Ridge Parkway between mileposts 170 and 171. From **Roanoke,** take the Blue Ridge Parkway south. Five miles south of Rte. 8, turn left off the parkway onto Rte. 720 and go 300 yards to the winery. **Coming north on the Blue Ridge Parkway,** 6.2 miles north of Rte. 58 turn right off the parkway onto Rte. 720 and go 1/2 mile to the winery.

Phone: 540-593-3100
E-mail: chianti@swva.net
Website: www.villaappalaccia.com

Tasting fee: None

Wines: Sangiovese, *Toscanello* (Cabernet Franc/Sangiovese), *Francesco* (Cabernet Franc), Pinot Grigio, *Lirico* (Vidal Blanc), *Simpatico* (Malvasia Bianca)

Wine related items for sale? Yes
Picnic area? Yes
Food available? Light snacks

Owners: Stephen Haskill and Susanne Becker
Winemakers/Viticulturists: Stephen Haskill and Susanne Becker

Before successful vintages of Chardonnay and Pinot Noir enabled them to vint a sparkling wine using the *cuvée* of choice of the French, winemakers in the United States produced "champagne" from the American hybrid Catawba. Making a traditional American sparkling wine was what Susanne Becker and Stephen Haskill had in mind when they planted Catawba vines in the 1980s. But the climate at 3,600 feet, the highest elevation of any winery in Virginia, would not let them bring the grapes to the kind of maturity that was needed. The acre of Catawbas now goes into the jams and jellies of a friend who produces them commercially.

Villa Appalaccia currently gets all its grapes from another tract of land it owns situated at a more vine-friendly 1,600 feet. The vineyards, however, are about twenty miles away. To ensure that the newly picked grapes retain their fresh, fruity characteristics, they are put in cold storage overnight at a nearby apple orchard then hauled to the winery early the next morning for crushing and pressing.

Wines that are crisp and long on fruit are essential to the Italian style of winemaking of Susanne and Stephen. Neither can claim a vestige of Italian heritage: she's of Finnish and Swedish extraction, and he's Anglo-Canadian. They just happen to be very partial to Italian foods and wines and after dropping Catawba bubbly from their plans, concentrated on growing Italian varieties. After a long and winding drive up the dirt and gravel road, you will find that you've arrived at Tuscany in the Appalachians, where the sign reads, "Virginia's Italian Wines—Sangiovese, Malvasia, Moscato, Pinot Grigio, Trebbiano"—plus some Vidal, Chardonnay, and Cabernet Franc. "At one point," says Susanne, "we were the fifth largest Sangiovese vineyard in the U.S., having only two acres."

Right now they have a total of twelve acres in the above-mentioned eight varieties, from which they produce anywhere from 3,000 to 4,000 cases annually, depending on the vintage. Susanne doesn't see them getting much bigger than that, partly because both she and husband Stephen have other jobs, he as a professor of cell biology and she doing immunology research for the Environmental Protection Agency. They also want to maintain the small winery traits implied in the name *Villa*. While travelling in Italy they met many interesting winemakers at some very small establishments. "Small vineyards and small winemaking are very common in Italy," Susanne explains. "Almost everybody does it." One farmer they met in Asti (of Asti Spumante fame) invited them to dinner, during which he brought out one delicious homemade wine after another. When asked to be shown the winery where these wonderful wines were being made, he took the couple to the vineyard instead. "Here," he proclaimed with gracious modesty, "is where the wine is made. You cannot make bad wine from good grapes." This might not be entirely true, Susanne notes, but at least, she adds, "if you do it the right way, you can make good wine from good grapes."

The incredibly good wines that Villa Appalaccia is making are, in the manner of the Italians, mostly blends. Their Sangiovese varietal is made in the Chianti fashion by barrel-fermenting this grape to dryness then adding small percentages of two whites, Malvasia and Trebbiano, and fermenting again. A light, aromatic, fruit-laden red is the result. Their *Toscanello* mixes Cabernet Franc and Sangiovese to create a "Super-Tuscan"—an Italian term—with full body and intense flavor.

The wines are poured at a solid mahogany bar in the tasting room amid muted earth tones and cool breezes. Although it's Virginia, this high up there's no need for air conditioning, even in summer. While in Italy, Susanne commissioned an artist in Orvieto to create a harvest scene and a winery scene. The medieval depictions, hand-painted on tiles in shades of turquoise and persimmon, brighten the wall on either side of the bar. Details from the paintings are charmingly reproduced on the winery's labels. Villa Appalaccia's Italian wines are modestly priced at $8.50 to $14.00 per bottle. The intrepid may inquire about the price of the Italian pottery in the glass cases.

On the portico, brick-lined arches frame scenes of mountain solitude, like the slow-moving silhouettes on "cow hill" against a sunset sky. Outside, picnic tables are placed right up against the woods, where unseen wilderness fauna can be heard making loud rustlings in the underbrush. As for the villa itself, the best view belongs to the cows. But as you approach the winery, from the pasture gate at the top of the hill you can see what they see—a little bit of Italy tucked serenely among the Blue Ridge Mountains.

More Virginia Wineries

As this book goes to press, Virginia has sixty-one licensed farm wineries that offer wine for sale on premises. Their wines may also be sold at local restaurants and retail outlets, or through other distribution channels. Included here are those wineries that were new and unvisited at the time this guide was published. Wineries which at present do not produce any wine from grapes are also included here, as are those that are open to visitors on a limited basis, or by appointment only.

Abingdon Vineyard and Winery: *Scheduled to open June 1, 2001.* 20530 Alvarado Road, Abingdon, VA 24211. Phone 540-623-1255. Open Friday through Sunday from noon to 6:00 p.m. Wines include Chardonel, Traminette, Cabernet Franc, Riesling, and red and white blends. Southwest Region

Amrhein's Wine Cellar: 9243 Patterson Drive, Bent Mountain, VA 24059. Phone: 540-387-3816. Fax: 540-387-1869. Wines include Cabernet Franc, Chambourcin, and blended white wines. Future vintages will include Viognier, a rosé, and *Tuscany Valley*. Southwest Region

Autumn Hill Vineyards/Blue Ridge Winery: 301 River Drive, Stanardsville, VA 22973. Phone: 804-985-6100. E-mail: autumnhill@mindspring.com. Offers tours, tastings, and special programs on weekends at various times throughout the year. (Confirm schedule in current Festival and Tour Guide.) Closed rest of the year. List includes Chardonnay, Riesling, Cabernets Franc and Sauvignon, and Merlot. Central Region

Boundary Rock Farm & Vineyard: 414 Riggins Road, Willis, VA 24380. Phone: 540-789-7098. Tours and tastings by appointment. Producing small lots from premium varieties, such as Cabernet Franc, Chardonnay, Riesling, Chambourcin, Vidal, Seyval, Traminette, Norton, and Cayuga. Southwest Region

Chrysalis Vineyards: 23876 Champe Ford Road, Middleburg, VA 20117. Phone: 800-235-8804, 540-687-8222. Fax: 540-687-8666. E-mail: info@chrysaliswine.com. Website: www.chrysaliswine.com. Open daily from 10:00 a.m. to 5:00 p.m. Vinifera plantings include the tried and true and several lesser known but intriguing European varieties, such as Tempranillo and Petit Manseng. Northern Region

Cooper Vineyards: 13372 Shannon Hill Road, Louisa, VA 23093. Phone: 540-894-5253. Fax: 804-285-8773. Open Saturdays from 11:00 a.m. to 5:00 p.m., Tuesdays from 3:00 p.m. to 5:00 p.m., and most Sundays. Other times, call for appointment. Wines include Cabernet Sauvignon, Chardonnay, Viognier, and *Electric Harvest Red*. Central Region

Glenway Winery: *Scheduled to open summer of 2001.* 14437 Hume Road, Huntly, VA 22630. Phone 540-635-9398. Open 11:00 a.m. to 5:00 p.m. Thursday through Monday. List includes vinifera varietals—Chardonnay, Cabernet, and Viognier—as well as wines made from French-American hybrids and native Virginia grapes. Northern Region

Guilford Ridge Vineyard: 328 Running Pine Road, Luray, VA 22835. Phone: 540-778-3853, 202-554-0333 (DC metro). Al fresco group tastings given on federal holiday weekends. Advance reservations required, and minimum party is 8 adults, or call to see if you can join a scheduled group. Estate-bottled releases include a Bordeaux-style red, a Beaujolais-style red, a late harvest red, and a crisp white wine. Shenandoah Valley Region

James River Wine Cellars: *Scheduled to open on June 1, 2001.* 11008 Washington Highway, Glen Allen, VA 23059. Phone: 804-550-7516. Fax: 804-550-1869. E-mail: winecellars@jrgm.com. Hours are 11:00 a.m. to 5:00 p.m. from Wednesday through Sunday. Closed major holidays and December 15 through March 15. Chardonnay, Chardonel, Gewürztraminer, Merlot, and Cabernet Sauvignon make up the inaugural list of Virginia wines being offered by this, the closest winery to the capital city of Richmond. Eastern Region

The Kluge Estate Winery and Vineyard: *Scheduled to open in the summer of 2002.* 3740 Blenheim Road, Charlottesville, VA 22902. Phone: 804-977-3895 (x55). Fax: 804-977-0606. E-mail ralmnt@aol.com. This winery will offer Grand Meritage (blend of Bordeaux wines) and Virginia sparkling wine. Vineyard tours and lectures are currently being conducted. Call for appointment. Central Region

Misty Mountain Vineyard and Winery: HCR 02, Box 459, Madison, VA 22727. Phone: 540-923-4378. Tours offered year round by appointment only. Producing Cabernet Sauvignon, Riesling, and Chardonnay. Central Region

Peaks of Otter Winery: 2122 Sheep Creek Road, Bedford, VA 24523. Phone: 540-586-3707. E-mail: appleseed@earthlink.net. Website: www.peaksofotterwinery.com. Open daily, 8:00 a.m. to 5:00 p.m. from August through November. Producing traditional and non-traditional fruit wines, including apple, peach, cherry, plum, crab apple, nectarine, and apple chili pepper! Southwest Region

Rose Bower Vineyard and Winery: P.O. Box 126 Hampden-Sydney, VA 23943. Phone: 804-223-8209. Tours and tastings by appointment only. Open for sales noon until 5:00 p.m. Tuesday through Sunday from March 15 through December 15. Estate-bottled wines, featuring Virginia Chardonnay. Central Region

Smokehouse Winery: 10 Ashby Road, Sperryville, VA 22740. Phone: 540-987-3194. Fax: 540-987-8189. E-mail: smokehouse@tidalwave.net. Website: smokehousewinerybnb.com. Open on weekends from 11:00 a.m. to 6:00 p.m., or by appointment. Closed Thanksgiving, Christmas, and New Year's. Produces traditional and non-traditional meads (honey wines), plus English-style, cask-served, "seasonal" hard cider. Central Region

Glossary

Here are some of the wine-related terms you will encounter in this book and at the wineries. If you do not find a term you are looking for here, check the index for a text reference.

Bordeaux reds. Varieties of *Vitis vinifera* for which the Bordeaux region of France is famous. They include Cabernet Franc, Cabernet Sauvignon, Malbec, Merlot, and Petit Verdot.

Brix. A standard measure of the sugar content, by weight, of grape juice or wine.

Brut. A dry sparkling wine.

Bud break. The beginning of the new cycle of life for a grapevine, when the first leaves emerge from their protective casings, or buds, in early spring.

Bung. A semi-conical plug, usually made of wood or silicone, designed to fit snugly in the hole of an oak barrel to keep oxygen from entering and to prevent wine from escaping through evaporation.

Carboy. A large glass jug.

Crush. Harvest time—when the grapes are picked, crushed, pressed, and the juice fermented—lasting roughly from mid-August to mid-October.

Crush pad. A cement- or concrete-paved area outside the winery where the grapes are brought during harvest (crush) to be crushed and/or pressed.

Crusher/destemmer. A piece of equipment that breaks the skins of the grapes and then separates them from their stems, in preparation for fermenting, or for pressing and then fermenting.

Destemmer/crusher. A piece of equipment that performs the same functions as a crusher/destemmer, but in reverse order.

Dry wine. Wine that has been allowed to ferment until all the sugar has been converted to alcohol.

Enology. The study of winemaking. Also spelled *oenology*.

Enophile. A wine lover. Also spelled *oenophile*.

European grapes. Generally speaking, grapes belonging to the species *Vitis vinifera*—from which the classic wines of Europe have been made for more than 2,000 years—as distinguished from native American varieties or grapes hybridized from American and European varieties.

Fine. To clarify, or to remove or attenuate certain components in the wine by filtration or other methods, such as egg whites.

Finished wine. Wine that has finished fermenting and aging and is, in the winemaker's judgment, ready to be bottled.

Gravity-flow system. A system that, to varying degrees, uses gravity—rather than pumps or other mechanical means—to move the grapes, the must, and the wine from one step in the winemaking process, or from one area within the winery, to another.

Late harvest. A sweet wine made from grapes that have been picked later in the season than the rest of the crop and therefore have developed a higher concentration of sugar.

Lees. Solids, including expired yeast cells, that settle to the bottom of a vessel—oak barrel or stainless steel tank—during fermentation and barrel aging.

Mead. A wine made by fermenting honey mixed with water.

Meritage. A trademark of the Meritage Association of California, used to describe a blend of the classic Bordeaux reds Cabernet Sauvignon, Cabernet Franc, and Merlot.

Must. The unfermented mixture of the juice, pulp, and skins of crushed grapes.

Punching down. Resubmerging—by hand with the aid of a stick, paddle, or similar device—the cap of skins and seeds that rises to the top of the vessel during fermentation.

Racking. Pumping or siphoning of the wine from one vessel into another to move it off the lees.

Still wine. Wine that has finished fermenting or whose fermentation has been deliberately halted to preserve some of the sugar; a noneffervescent wine, as opposed to a sparkling wine, such as champagne.

Tannin. A compound found in the skins, seeds, and stems of grapes, as well as the oak barrels in which they are fermented and/or aged. It gives wine, especially red wine, its slightly astringent quality. Most of the tannin in wine comes from the grape skins and the barrels.

Terroir. A French word meaning soil, often used by winegrowers to mean the overall conditions—climate, soil, geography—in which a grape is grown. Wine grapes are very sensitive to their terroir, and thus a wine's personality is the result of its heredity and environment, not to mention the influence of the winemaker.

Varietal. A bottled wine bearing the name of only one variety of grape, e.g., "Chardonnay." Under federal regulations, a wine must contain at least 75 percent by volume of wine made from the named variety in order to qualify as a varietal.

Vigneron. A winegrower or viticulturist (French).

Vineyard designated. A wine, usually a varietal, made with grapes from a specific vineyard, which is identified on the label.

Viniculture. The art and science of making wine.

Vinify. To turn into wine.

Vint. To produce an alcoholic beverage by the process of fermentation alone (as opposed to brewing or distilling).

Vintage year. The year in which the grapes were picked. In order to qualify as a vintage wine, 95 percent of the wine in the bottle must come from grapes harvested in the year designated on the label.

Viticulture. The art and science of growing grapes.

Bibliography

Cox, Jeff. *From Vines to Wines: The Complete Guide to Growing Grapes and Making Your Own Wine.* 3d ed. Pownal, Vermont: Storey Books, 1999.

Gabler, James M. *Passions: The Wines and Travels of Thomas Jefferson.* Baltimore: Bacchus Press, 1995.

Johnson, Hugh. *Vintage: The Story of Wine.* New York: Simon and Schuster, 1989.

———. *The World Atlas of Wine.* Rev. ed. New York: Simon and Schuster, 1978.

Kennedy, Frances H., ed. *The Civil War Battlefield Guide.* Boston: Houghton Mifflin, 1990.

Lawrence, R. de Treville III, ed. *Jefferson and Wine: Model of Moderation.* 2d ed. The Plains, Virginia: The Vinifera Wine Growers Association, Inc., 1989.

Lee, Hilde Gabriel and Allan E. Lee. *Virginia Wine Country.* White Hall, Virginia: Betterway Publications, 1987.

———. *Virginia Wine Country Revisited.* 2nd printing (updated). Charlottesville, Virginia: Hildesigns Press, 1995.

Thomas, Marguerite. *Wineries of the Eastern States.* 3d ed. Lee, Massachusetts: Berkshire House Publications, 1999.

The Virginia Wine Marketing Program. *Virginia Wineries Festival and Tour Guide 2001.* Richmond. Published annually. A free current guide is available at the wineries or by writing or calling the Wine Marketing Office at P.O. Box 1163, Richmond, VA 23218, 800-828-4637.

Winkler, A. J., J[ames] A. Cook, W. M. Kliewer, and L[loyd] A. Lider. *General Viticulture.* Rev. ed. Los Angeles: University of California Press, 1974.

Index

Abingdon Vineyard and Winery, 124
Adair, Shelly, 4
Adlum, John, 67
Afton Mountain Vineyards, 14-15
Alexander (grape), 11
Allen, Marlyn and Sue, 26
American hybrids, see under *grapes*
Amrhein's Wine Cellar, 124
Archer, Gabriel, 66-67
Armor, David, 48-49; Marilyn, 48
aroma, 79
aroma wheel, see organoleptic chart
Autumn Hill Vineyards, 124
Barber, David, 79
Barbour, James, 16
Barboursville Vineyards, 11, 16-19, 20, 50
barrels, oak, 14, 17, 21, 102
Bazaco, George, 92; Hope, 92-93; Nicki, 92
Beaujolais, 71, 79
Becker, Susanne, 122-123
Belcher, Clyde, 112
Bell, Graham, 28-29
Bieda, Joan, 28
blanc de noir, 104
Blessing of the Vines, 88
Bordeaux mixture, 85
Bordeaux region, 23, 32, 60, 97
Botrytis, 85
Boundary Rock Farm and Vineyard, 124
bouquet, 79
Breaux, Alexis, 72; Madeleine, 72; Paul, 72-73
Breaux Vineyards, 72-73, 100
Breiner, Al, 50-51; Chris, 50
Brix, 55
brut, 87
bubbler, 44, 59
bud, 24
bud break, 20, 64, 110
bunch rot, see Botrytis
bung, 59
Burgin, Bob, 112, 114
Burnley Vineyards, 20-21
Burroughs, Rick, 110-111
Cabernet Franc, 16
callusing room, 82
canes, 20, 82
canopy management, 64
capsule, 25

carbon dioxide, 44, 59
Champ, Antony and Edith, 54-55
Charlottesville, 12, 32
Château Lafite, 33
Château Morrisette, 112-115
Chobanian, Matt, 60-61
Chrysalis Vineyards, 124
cider, hard, 94-95
Civil War, 11-12, 65, 76-77, 83, 109, 52-53, 71
claret, Virginia, 11
cold filtration, 38, 43
cold soaking, 48
Collins, David, 72
Cooper Vineyards, 124
cork, 38
Corpora, Shinko, 14-15; Tom, 14-15
Crider, Walter, 118
crop thinning, 64, 80
Cruden, D. Scott, 54
crusher/destemmer, 14, 21, 62, 76
cuvée, 87, 122
Davis, Bart, 52-53; Larry and Sterry, 52
Deer Meadow Vineyard, 104-105
destemmer, 39
Dodd's Cider Mill, 94-95
Dom Pérignon, abbot, 38; champagne, 87
Dominion Wine Cellars, 22-23
dosage, 87
downy mildew, 85
dressing, of wine bottles, 25
Duffeler, Patrick, 4, 22-23, 66, 68; Peggy, 66
Dye, John, 116; Ken and Linda, 116-117
Dye's Vineyards and Winery, 116-117
egg whites, for fining, 33
Everette, Dave, 4
Fabian, Hans, 90
Farfelu Vineyards, 74-75
Farm Wineries Act, 34, 128
Federweisse, 44
fermentation, 8, 33, 44, 55, 58-59, 90
filtering, of yeast, 91
fining, 33, 80
Fitter, John, 90-91
Flemer, Carl, 60-62; Doug, 60-61; Shirley, 62
Foster, Brad and Krista, 108

fox grapes, 28
foxy, 9
Franco, Fernando, 16
Franklin, Benjamin, 32, 42
free-run, 76, 120
French hybrids, 11
French-American hybrids, see French hybrids
Furness, Elizabeth, 90
Furr, Jim, 74
gallons vs. cases, 15
Glenway Winery, 124
gondola, 21
grafting, 11, 82
graft joint (union), 39, 72, 82
Grant, Ulysses S., 52, 76
grape growing, by English settlers, 9-10; history in Virginia, 9-12; at Jamestown, 9-10; at Williamsburg, 10, 12, 66-67
grapes, American hybrids, 10-11; flavor mimicry, 8, 81; French hybrids, 11; native American, 9; propagation of, 11, 82; *Vitis vinifera,* 9-12
gravity-flow system, 14, 26, 74, 104, 120
Gray Ghost, see Mosby, John Singleton
Gray Ghost Winery, 76-77
Grayhaven Winery, 24-25
Griffin, Judy, 4
Guilford Ridge Vineyard, 124
Hanchey, Neal, 4
Hanson, Ella, 42; Richard, 42-43
Harper, Phoebe, 84; Robert (Bob), 84
Harris, Cathy, 94; John, 94-95
Hartwood Winery, 78-79
Haskill, Stephen, 122
Heidig, Ann, 64; Bill, 64; Eric, 64; Jeff, 64
Henry, Patrick, 71
Hill, Chris, 32
Hill Top Berry Farm, 26-27
Hollerith, Joachim, 46
Horton, Dennis, 28-29; Sharon, 28
Horton Cellars Winery, 28-31
Hubert, Margaret, 98; R. J. (Whitie), 98-99
Hurricane Camille, 58
Hurricane Fran, 22
Ingleside Plantation Vineyards, 60-63
Jackson, John, 108-109

126

Jackson, Stonewall, 65, 109
James River Wine Cellars, 124
Jamestown, 9-10, 66
Jefferson, Thomas, 3, 10-13, 16-18, 23, 32-33, 50, 67
Jefferson Vineyards, 32-33, 50
Jeffersonian Wine Grape Growers Society, 37
Kanev, Svetlozar, 42-43
Keckley, Garry, 61
Kellert, Al, 76-77; Amy, 77; Cheryl, 76-77
Kluge Estate Winery and Vineyard, The, 124
Lake Anna Winery, 64-65
Landwirt Vineyard, 106-107
Law, Jim, 64, 80-81, 100
Lecomte, Alain, 40
Leducq, Jean, 38, 40
Lee, Robert E., 52-53, 60, 65
lees, 44, 87
Linden Vineyards, 64, 80-81, 100
Livingston, Beverly, 78-79; Jim, 78-79
Loudoun Valley Vineyards, 82-83
Löwentraut, Frank, 90
lug, 21, 99
Magruder, Mark, 42
malmsey, 18
malolactic conversion (fermentation), 13, 48, 59, 76, 90
Malvasia, 18
Mazzei, Filippo, 10, 22-23, 32, 50
McCarthy, Brad, 54
McCormack, Dick, 108
McCoy, Ken, Jr. and Ken, Sr., 46-47
mead, 26, 47, 52, 118
mechanical harvester, 22, 39
Medaglia, Corky, 118-119; Nancy, 118
Meredyth Vineyards, 11, 34, 128
Meritage, 87-88
méthode champenoise, 25, 87
Michie Tavern, 32, 37
microclimate, 12
Misty Mountain Vineyard and Winery, 124
ML, see malolactic conversion
Monticello, 10, 32, 50
Monticello viticultural appellation, 37
Morrisette, David, 112-114; William and Nancy, 112
Morton, Lucie, 78
Mosby, John Singleton, 71, 76-77, 83

Mountain Cove Vineyards, 34-35
Muncy, Bruce, 4
must, 14
Naked Mountain Vineyard, 84-85
netting, as defense against birds, 25
nitrogen, 38
noble rot, see Botrytis
North Mountain Vineyard and Winery, 108-109
Norton (grape), 11, 21, 28-29, 34
nose, see bouquet
Oakencroft Vineyard and Winery, 36-37
Oasis Winery, 11, 86-89
organoleptic chart, 81
Osborne, Caroline, 74-75; John, 74-75
Palladio, Andrea, 17
Parker, Amy, 102-103; Lew, 102-103
Paschina, Luca, 16-19
Payette, Amy Kellert, 77; Tom, 38-40
Peaks of Otter Winery, 124
Pearmund, Chris, 74-75, 100
Peple, Charles and Lyn, 24-25
Pérignon, see Dom Pérignon
phylloxera, in America, 9-10; in France, 11
Piedmont Vineyards and Winery, 11, 90-91
Ponton, Philip, 36
port wine, 28
press, barrel, 43; bladder, 43, 55, 61
Prince Michel de Virginia, 20, 38-41
prohibition, national, 11, 28, 94; in Virginia, 11, 94;
punching down, 33, 80, 120
racking, 44, 91, 106, 121
Randel, Emma, 110-111; Jim, 110
Raney, Charles, 74-75; Virginia, 75
Rapidan River Vineyards, 39
Rausse, Gabriele, 50
Rebec Vineyards, 42-43
Recht, Jacques, 60-61; Liliane, 60
Reeder, C. J., 20; Dawn, 20-21; Lee, 20-21; Patt, 20
reserve wine, 61, 76
residual sugar, 65
Riddick, Kathy, 58; Mike, 58
riddling, 87
Ridgeway, Linda, 91
Rigby, Stephen, 60-61
Rocchiccioli, Judith, 70; Kathryn, 70; Randy, 70

Rockbridge Vineyard, 44-45
Rogan, Felicia Warburg, 36-37; John, 36
rootstock, 11, 82
Rose Bower Vineyard and Winery, 124
Rose River Vineyards, 46-47
Rouse, Jane, 44; Shepherd, 44-45
sabrage, **88**
Salahi, Corinne, 86; Dirgham, 86; Tareq, 86-88
Sarle, Charles and Jennifer, 104-105
scion, 72, 82
Sémillon, 91
Shadwell-Windham Winery, 92-93
Shaps, Michael, 32-33, 36
Sharp Rock Vineyards, 48-49
Shenandoah Vineyards, 110-111
Shiraz, see Syrah
shoot, 20, 64, 82
Simeon Vineyards, 32
Simmers, Gary, 106-107; Teresa, 106
Simmons, Terry, 4
Smith, Archie, Jr., 34, 128; Archie, III, 128
Smith, Captain John, 60, 66
Smokehouse Winery, 124
sparkling wine, 39, 87
Spotted Tavern Winery, 94-95
Steuben (grape), 104-105
Stone, Jeff and Tamara, 58
Stone Mountain Vineyards, 50-51
Stonewall Vineyards and Winery, 52-53
Sullivan, Joe B. III, 84
Super-Tuscan, 123
sur lies, 106
Swedenburg Estate Vineyard, 96-97
Swedenburg, Juanita, 96; Wayne, 96-97
Syrah, 120
tannin, 12, 34-35, 55, 111
Tarara Vineyard and Winery, 98-99
tartrate crystals, 38, 43, 111
thermal inversion, 15, 20
Tomahawk Mill Winery, 118-119
Travers, Barbara, 4
Tucker, Dolores, 82; Hubert, 82
Unicorn Winery, 100-101
Valhalla Vineyards, 120-121
vanillin, 84
Vascik, Debra, 120-121; Jim, 120-121
vigneron, 10, 32
Vikings, 9
Villa Appalaccia Winery, 122-123

Vineland (Vinland), 9
vineyard designated, 80
Viognier, 28-29
Virginia Farm Wineries Act, see Farm Wineries Act
Virginia Tech, 10, 34, 100, 128
Virginia Winegrowers Advisory Board, 37
Virginia Wineries Association, 128
viticultural appellation, 37, 110
Vitis aestivalis, 10-11
Vitis labrusca, 10-11
Vitis riparia, 10-11, 25
Vitis rotundifolia, 10
Vitis vinifera, 9-13, 15
von Finck, Gerhard, 90
Warner, Steve, 22-23, 66
Washington, George, 60, 67, 84
water sources (as conduits for air circulation), 26, 75
Weed, A. C. (Al), 34-35, 128; Emily, 34
Weems, Thomas, 4
White Hall Vineyards, 54-57
Whittaker, David, 100-101
whole-berry pressing, see whole-cluster pressing
whole-cluster pressing, 13, 33, 55, 61, 76, 84
Williamsburg, 10, 12, 22-23, 44, 66-67
Williamsburg Winery, The, 22-23, 66-69
Willowcroft Farm Vineyards, 102-103
wind machines, 20
Windy River Winery, 70-71
wine, finished, 44; new, 44; still, 44, 87
Winiarski, Warren, 6
Wintergreen Winery, 58-59
Wolf, Tony, 48, 100
Woodward, Stanley, Jr., 32; Stanley, Sr., 32
yeast, 70; native (wild), 8, 33, 90, 94
Zinfandel, 21, 83
Zoecklein, Bruce, 34
Zonin, Giovanni, 16

Meredyth Vineyards, Middleburg

It can easily be said that the visionary spirit—and indeed the entrepreneurial daring—that created Meredyth Vineyards was the leaven that gave rise to Virginia's modern wine industry. It was in the living room of Meredyth's founder, Archie Smith, Jr., that the Virginia Wineries Association was formed in the mid-seventies with a charter membership of five forward-looking winegrowers. In 1980 Smith and a young winery owner named Al Weed worked with a member of the House of Delegates to draft the basics of a very progressive and industry-supportive piece of legislation that became known as the Virginia Farm Wineries Act. Over the years the viticultural and enological programs at Virginia Tech both benefited from Meredyth's willingness to be a test site for a number of wine-related studies.

Archie Smith III was the winemaker here from the time the winery opened in 1975 until its closing in the year 2000. Like his father, he was a leader in the Virginia wine industry throughout his entire career. Before becoming a full-time winemaker, he had earned advanced degrees in philosophy at Oxford and subsequently held a teaching position there. During the frequent six-week breaks in the English academic year, he would return to Middleburg to make wine and tend the vines. In 1975, while Archie was still its part-time winemaker, Meredyth Vineyards pressed its first vintage and received its winery license. In 1976, the year of the bicentennial, the Smiths took their 1975 Villard Blanc to the Yorktown Victory Center, where the public—after a forced abstinence spanning more than sixty years—was once again able to taste a commercially produced Virginia wine.

Meredyth's list was long and inclusionary: Archie treated vinifera and hybrid with equal respect, and the grapes responded with wines that across the board reflected what would ultimately be a quarter century spent fine tuning a remarkable winemaking talent.

Some of the state's most beautiful countryside was to be experienced at Meredyth Vineyards. The stone ruins of an old tenant dwelling became one of the most photographed and recognized landmarks in Virginia wine country. In the enduring memory one has of this place, vine-ribboned hills rise and dip, riding the ancient geologic currents towards the Bull Run Mountains in the distance. On a clear evening late in September, a glow appears behind the mountains in the east. As you watch it growing in intensity, suddenly, framed within the ebony silhouette of the ruins, a harvest moon—bigger than you've ever seen it, as bright and orange as a wheel of ripe cheddar—glides up silently to perch momentarily atop the mountain. Rising rapidly, the full moon changes from orange to yellow to brilliant white, and soon the hills, the vines, and the ruins are bathed in a soft and almost mystical light.

Friends of this venerable winery will miss its singularly beautiful surroundings, its uniquely excellent wines, and its truly inimitable winemaker. Its closing surely marks the end of an era in Virginia's modern winemaking history. But just as a portion of the original leaven is to be found in every new loaf of bread, some of the founding spirit of Meredyth Vineyards will be at work in each new winery that opens its doors in what is fast becoming Virginia's golden age of wine.